I0169622

POSITIVIKEY

THE KEY TO HAPPINESS

A GUIDE TO LIVING A

Positive Life

IN 10 KEY STEPS

Nicco Boss

Disclaimer:

The information provided in this book is to be used for instructional and motivational purposes only. The recommendations made are not intended to diagnose or prescribe for medical or psychological conditions, or to substitute for the medical advice of a qualified healthcare provider. It is strictly meant to provide information amassed from the education, research, and experience of the author. It is distributed with the understanding that the publisher and author are not engaged in rendering psychological, health, legal, financial, career, or other professional services. If expert assistance or counseling is needed, the services of a professional should be sought. The author is not a lawyer, doctor, or mental health professional, so please use your best judgement always when applying information from this book into your own life.

Although every precaution has been taken to verify the accuracy of the information contained herein, the author and publisher assume no responsibility for any errors or omissions. No liability is assumed for damages that may result from the use of information contained within.

Copyright © 2016 by Nicco Boss, LLC

All Rights Reserved

PositiviKEY Publications

ISBN 978-0-9891635-9-0

www.NiccoBoss.com

INTRODUCTION

I would like to extend my deepest gratitude to you for taking an interest in reading my book and investing your time in applying the techniques I describe. It is my sincere belief that, in making a conscious effort to follow the steps outlined here, you will find the happiness you seek and truly deserve.

Happiness is the one thing that all people want, yet can't seem to sustain on a lasting basis. But why is persistent happiness so elusive? We all know what it feels like to be happy, so why can't we maintain that feeling all the time? It's because happiness is not a perpetual condition; rather, it's a state of well-being derived from cumulative moments of collective purpose.

We can't be floating on a cloud every minute of every day — that would be unrealistic. If we didn't encounter sadness, we would never be able to appreciate the feeling of genuine contentment. The contrast of emotions makes it possible for us to experience what it is to be human. The purpose of our existence is not to be happy all the time, but to aspire to a life full of meaning.

When you uncover the meaning of your reality, you tip the scales toward a life of positivity, both in outlook and in outcome. When you can achieve this, you won't have to look for happiness — happiness will find you!

How can you discover meaning and positivity? Follow the Ten Keys I've detailed in this book, and you will quickly be on your way to accomplishing this goal, and to finding profound, long-lasting happiness.

Happiness Always!

Nicco Boss

C*ontents*

Nicco Boss

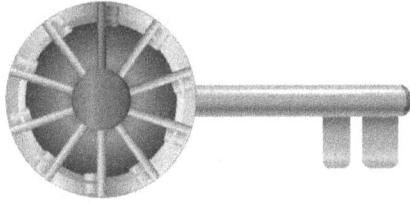

1

BELIEVE IN YOURSELF
AND YOU CAN MAKE ANYTHING HAPPEN

"In order to succeed, we must first believe that we can."
~Nikos Kazantzakis

Believing in yourself is the first key to success. When you believe in yourself, you eliminate doubt. When you have no doubt, you erase fear. And when you feel no fear, you become unstoppable! Believe in yourself and you will be able to accomplish anything you set your mind to.

I know it's difficult to believe in yourself when, for the better part of your life, you've been doing just the opposite.

Think of how many times you've told yourself, "I'm not good enough/ strong enough/ good-looking enough;" or, "I'm not as smart as other people;" or, "I'll never amount to anything." And how many times have you believed these things you tell yourself? Most likely, every time. So why is it so easy to believe negative things about ourselves, but not positive things? It's because we've been programmed to think a certain way.

When we are born, our brains are a clean slate, free of opinions, beliefs, attitudes, fears, and hatred. But quite literally, our brains are sponges, and from the time we enter the world, we begin absorbing information which effectively "hardwires" our gray matter. Our upbringing, environment, experiences, culture, religion, and more fill our minds and help shape our thinking. Unfortunately, many of our life experiences are not positive, and our belief system is a reflection of that. In today's world, we are bombarded with socially constructed images of beauty and standards of success, which are practically unachievable in reality. However, people (especially the impressionable youth), compare themselves to fabricated examples of perfection. In doing so, they see that they can't measure up and they end up feeling like utter failures. It's no wonder that more people nowadays are suffering from depression than ever before!

In order to see ourselves in a positive light and to start believing in ourselves, we must change our thinking, and the only way to do that is to reprogram our thought processes. We can literally change our habits and beliefs by rewiring our brains. In recent years, a great deal of attention has been focused on neuroplasticity, which is the brain's ability to reorganize itself by forming new synaptic connections throughout life. Neuroplasticity enables neurons (nerve cells) to compensate for disease and injury. The brain's neural synapses and pathways can also be altered in response to new situations and resulting from environmental, behavioral, and neural changes. By adopting a new method of thinking, we can indisputably "change our minds" — in the best sense! (More on neuroplasticity in Key 6.)

Most people don't realize what a powerful tool the mind is. Mental strength can be much stronger than the physical. Unfortunately, most of us don't take the time to build our mental muscle. Often, people think that a strong mind comes from filling our brains with lots of (usually unimportant) information. Ironically, our minds become strong by clearing out all of the static.

One way to silence the noise in our heads is to meditate. If you feel like that sounds too New Age or mystical, try considering meditation as a "time-out" to recharge. Just as you need to close out tabs on your computer or recharge the batteries on your electronics for better functionality, you must also take steps to re-energize yourself, or you will surely crash and burn out.

If it helps you to relate, think of meditation as a "mini-vacation." Just as when you're on vacation, you are allowed to relax and not feel guilty about it, meditation affords you the opportunity to self-indulgently get away from it all — even if it's only for a short time. So if it feels weird to say, "I'm going to meditate," instead declare, "I'm taking a mini-vacay!" Allow yourself to go to that tropical beach paradise, snowy mountaintop hideaway, or wildflower-filled meadow. If you picture yourself at a beautiful destination, it will be that much easier to get into a meditative or — if you'd prefer — "mini-vacay" state of mind.

When you meditate, you are relaxing the body and calming the mind. On a fundamental level, meditating involves bringing awareness to the present moment — done most easily by focusing on your breathing — which prevents you from being distracted by worries, fears, problems, etc. Since breathing is an unconscious function of the autonomic nervous system, most people don't pay attention to it, leading to shallow, incomplete breaths. But when you consciously take a deep breath, let it fill your body, and hold it in for a few seconds, you instantly feel the life force that it holds. Equally powerful, when you fully release the breath upon exhaling, you can sense the negative energy being released and a surge of fortitude flooding your body. If you don't believe it, try taking a few deep breaths and exhaling completely. I promise, you'll feel the difference immediately.

Just imagine what regular meditation (basically, practiced breathing and relaxation) can do for you. There are numerous advantages, but if you still feel reluctant to try it, here are a few of the benefits you'll get out of quieting your mind:

- Meditation reduces stress. Stress increases cortisol production, which triggers inflammation in the body and also enlarges the amygdala, the part of the brain responsible for anxiety, fear, anger, and worry. As the amygdala grows in size, fear-based thought processing is augmented, creating a chronic "fight or flight" response. Deep-breathing meditation floods the brain with oxytocin (neurochemical that calms the stress response) and dramatically decreases cortisol output. As a result, anxiety, fear, and stress subside, and — in a short amount of time — the amygdala shrinks in size. Deep breathing meditation also helps to reduce the heart rate and combat your body's inflammatory response to stress by engaging the vagus nerve, which extends from the brain down through most major organs of the body (more on this to follow shortly and in Key 4). Heightened stress, accelerated heart rate, elevated cortisol levels, and increased inflammation are all contributors in the rising rates of illness. In today's world, we can all use a little (or a lot of) stress reduction. People of all ages are now feeling the pressures of our fast-paced and highly-demanding world. By reducing tension naturally with meditation, we can eliminate our reliance on prescription anti-anxiety medications. These drugs attack our bodies, leading to the need for other medications to repair the damage, which causes even more stress. It becomes a vicious, unhealthy cycle.

- Meditation encourages a healthy lifestyle. When you take toxins out of your body, you give it a chance to heal naturally. Meditation can curb cravings for cigarettes, alcohol, sugar, and processed foods, (and it can terminate the need for medications, such as those just referred to). I realize it's not easy to break lifelong habits, and some people will find it difficult to give up their sweet treats or other "rewards." But if you start meditating for just a few minutes every day, you'll find that, in no time, your cravings will diminish significantly and eventually disappear. You won't even miss those things you thought you couldn't live without, and you'll feel so much better!

- Meditation boosts cardiovascular health. People who meditate are less likely to have a heart attack or stroke. When practicing deep-breathing meditation, the compound nitric oxide is increased in the body. This causes blood vessels to open up, resulting in a lower heart rate and a drop in blood pressure. Improved oxygen flow in the body also clears toxins out of the blood, helping to combat the aging process!

- Meditation slows aging. A Harvard University study has shown that meditators have longer telomeres, the caps on chromosomes which indicate biological age. They're not promising a longer life, but I think that with less stress on the body and heart, it's a given. And looking good longer isn't a bad side-effect! In addition to building longer telomeres, meditation also influences three important age-affecting hormones: DHEA, melatonin, and cortisol. The production of DHEA, a potent anti-aging hormone which can guard against disease, is enhanced significantly with meditation. This is also true of melatonin, which — besides being a sleep hormone — is also a powerful antioxidant, antidepressant, and anti-aging agent. Cortisol, on the other hand, is a stress hormone which causes inflammation, thinning skin, and (as I mentioned before) an enlarged amygdala. But with regular meditation, you can cut cortisol production in half! (More on cortisol in Key 4.)

- Meditation increases the neurotransmitter dopamine, improving focus and concentration. Regular meditators experience deep relaxation, heightened creativity, and the improved ability to learn. In fact, all sorts of hobbies — including knitting, sewing, drawing, painting, photography, and woodworking — bring the brain into a meditative state. Any of these types of activities boost dopamine output, ward off depression, and protect the brain against aging.

- Meditation helps to keep you in the present moment. When you focus on the present, you are neither anxious over what may happen in the future, nor are you able to obsess over what has happened in the past. Being in the now allows you to be self-aware, causing growing acceptance of your own life and situation, as well as acceptance of others by way of a greater sense of empathy and compassion.

- ***MEDITATION INCREASES HAPPINESS*** by augmenting grey-matter density in brain structures responsible for self-awareness, introspection, and self-compassion. When you have the ability to stop time and really get a sense of *WHERE* you are and *WHO* you are, you are capable of seeing things more clearly. From this perspective, you are able to make sound decisions about where you are going. Sometimes all you need is clarity and direction. Meditation gives you these things, and then (as if by magic) the answers that you seek are all right there in front of you. The beauty of it is that the answers have been there *within you* all along, just waiting to be unlocked. Let meditation be your key!

Maybe you've tried meditating in the past, but you can't seem to do it because your mind just won't stop racing. That's all right. It's perfectly normal for thoughts to come into your head. The goal is to be able to acknowledge the thoughts and send them back out of your mind. To do this, focus on your breathing. It helps to count your breaths because your mind is occupied with counting, rather than with superfluous thoughts.

Concentrating on deep, rhythmic breath helps turn your attention inward and activates your parasympathetic (aka "rest and digest" or "tend and befriend") nervous system, promoting calm and relaxation. The main component of the parasympathetic nervous system is the *vagus nerve* (introduced earlier), which is the tenth cranial nerve and longest of the autonomic nervous system in the human body. It originates in the part of the brain stem called the medulla oblongata and wanders (*vagus* means "wandering" in Latin) all the way down to the colon, supplying nerve fibers to almost all of the organs in between, including the heart, lungs, and digestive tract.

In the first quarter of the 20th century, it was discovered that stimulating the vagus nerve slowed the heart rate by triggering the release of the neurotransmitter acetylcholine, which acts as a transmitter at all neuromuscular connections. Acetylcholine stimulates muscle movement, causing skeletal muscles to contract and — surprisingly — heart muscles to relax. Therefore, by activating the vagus nerve to produce acetylcholine, you can reduce your heart rate, create inner calm, and regulate your body's inflammatory reflex.

The vagus nerve is connected to oxytocin receptors, and keeping it healthy (or having a high "vagal tone") is directly related to a stronger immune system response. With a robust immune system, you are better equipped to fight stress and disease, and when you're healthier, you're happier! There are many ways to engage and strengthen your vagus nerve, including exercising, fasting, getting acupuncture, chanting *OM*, laughing, and singing. But arguably the most effective method of improving vagal tone is to meditate employing deep, diaphragmatic breathing with long, slow exhales.

If you've never meditated before, or you've attempted it but don't really know if you're doing it right, I have a simple and easy-to-do (yet very beneficial) meditation for you to try. You can do this every day for as long as you like: I suggest 10 to 20 minutes, once or twice a day. You'll be surprised at how relaxed, recharged, and positive you feel afterward. By clearing your mind of noise, doubt, and negativity, you open it up to promise, hope, and positivity. In doing this, you will be able to see clearly and focus on the good within you, which in turn will allow you to believe in yourself and your ability to achieve any goal you set out to accomplish. So let's begin:

MEDITATION EXAMPLE

Allow yourself at least ten minutes and find a place in your home away from excess noise. You can play soothing instrumental music if you wish, which helps to drown out noise — if you happen to live in a big city, for example. Sit on a soft surface (such as a yoga mat or blanket) with your legs crossed loosely, or you can sit in a comfortable position in a chair with your feet flat on the floor. The object is to feel as tranquil as possible. Relax your shoulders and arms, letting your hands rest on your thighs, palms up or down. Close your eyes gently and begin by taking one deep breath in through your nose, counting to four. Hold your breath for a count of four, and then exhale through your mouth to another count of four. Next, refrain from inhaling for four counts, and then begin the process once again. I call this my **Four Square Meditation**. When doing this, I picture a square:

```
                    ┌──── (2) Hold ────▷
          △         ┌─────────────────────┐         │
          │         │                     │         │
(1) Inhale│         │                     │         │(3) Exhale
          │         │                     │         │
          │         └─────────────────────┘         ▽
                    ◁──── (4) Hold ────┘
```

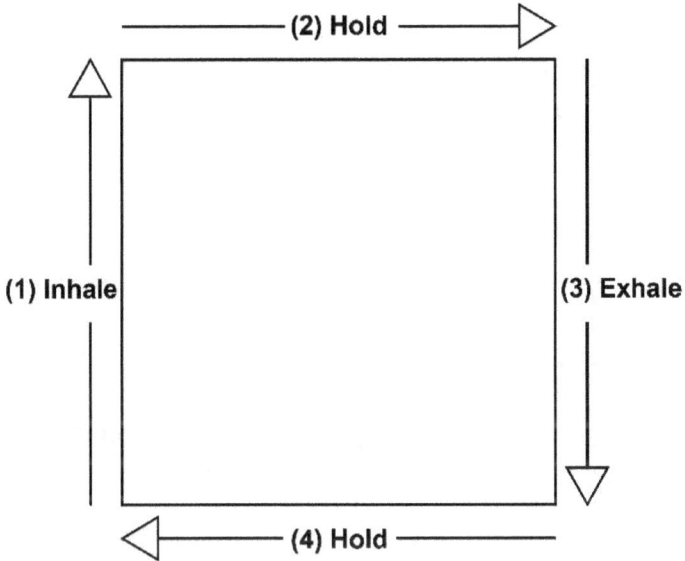

As I'm counting my breaths, I visualize traveling around the square, from the bottom left corner to the top left while inhaling to a count of four, and then holding the breath to a count of four while going from the top left corner to the top right. I exhale from the top right corner to the bottom right to a count of four and then refrain from breathing for four counts as I travel from the bottom right corner back across to the bottom left where I started. The act of counting while also envisioning traveling around the square helps to keep you focused and prevents distracting thoughts from entering your mind. Holding your breath improves your concentration on the task at hand, forcing you to pay attention to releasing or taking your next breath. In doing so, you don't think of anything else. Also, after holding your breath, your next exhalation feels great because you're releasing carbon dioxide, and your next inhalation is incredible because you are taking in oxygen, providing you with a burst of energy!

If you do this meditation for just minutes a day, you will notice a difference in how you feel. If you have more time, by all means take advantage of utilizing this healing technique! Do it in the morning after you wake up to energize yourself, and try it again before bedtime to help relax you and prepare you for a great night's sleep!

===

For more meditations, please visit my website:
www.NiccoBoss.com

===

To really believe in yourself, you must always remember to **BE YOU**:

*BE*lieve in

*YOU*rself

The quickest way to lose your identity is to compare yourself to others. Don't worry about what other people are doing, or how they present their lives to be. You have no idea what their journey is about. Focus on you: your strengths, your abilities, and your dreams. Be proud of who you are, what you have to offer, and what you have accomplished. Be yourself, because an original is always worth more than a copy. The only one you should be comparing yourself to or competing with is *you*. That means you should only strive to become better than the person you were yesterday.

You should know that, just as you observe others, wishing to have what they have or to be more like they are, other people are doing the same with you. You probably don't realize how many people look at you with admiration, respect, and maybe even a little envy. So be happy with who you are and how you look. Embrace all of your great qualities and unique features. *YOU* are responsible for creating your own happiness, and that starts within you. Happiness is an inside job. If you are looking outside yourself to find long-term happiness — in a relationship, with a job, from a car or a house or other possessions — you'll be searching forever. True happiness starts with a happy outlook and an appreciation for everything in life, big or small. It is only when you accept and love who you are that you will undoubtedly succeed in finding happiness. The foundation for this appreciation is gratitude, which is discussed in greater detail in Key 3.

To understand just how powerful believing in yourself can be, I'd like to relate a story about Two Frogs:

A group of frogs were hopping through the woods one day when two of them suddenly fell into a deep pit. All of the other frogs gathered around the hole to see if they could help their friends out. When they saw how deep the pit was, they came to dismal conclusions: "It's too deep … there's no way out!" A few lamented, "You'll never make it out alive!"

The two frogs decided to ignore the comments and attempted to jump out of the pit. They tried with all their might, but seemed to be getting nowhere. The frogs who were watching kept croaking louder and louder, telling the two that they might as well stop. They tried to convince them that they were wasting their time because they were as good as dead.

Finally, one of the two frogs heeded the pessimistic advice of the frogs watching from above. He quit jumping and literally "croaked" and died. The other frog kept on jumping as hard as he could in an attempt to avoid the fate of his fallen friend. Once again, the crowd of frogs yelled at him to quit jumping and save himself from all of the pain he was inflicting upon himself by leaping and falling back down to the bottom of the pit over and over again.

Still, the frog continued to jump, trying harder and harder as the other frogs shouted more and more for him to give up. Finally, with one last leap, he managed to make it out of the deep pit. It was then that the other frogs asked him, "Did you not hear us? Why did you keep jumping, even though we yelled at you to stop?" The frog looked at them and said, "I'm sorry, but I don't know what you are saying. You see, I'm deaf, but I'm very grateful that you cheered me on the whole time I was down there. Your encouragement helped me believe in myself."

So you see, believing in yourself is nothing more than having the right mindset. How you perceive is what you'll believe, achieve, and receive, and whatever you could ever need or desire is within you. If you want acceptance, accept yourself; if you want appreciation, appreciate yourself; and if you want "likes," like yourself! You are worthy of all of the best in life, and you are worth whatever you believe you are. So the key is to believe in yourself wholeheartedly! If you believe you can achieve something, then there really isn't anything to stop you from reaching your goal! And speaking of goals, read on to Key 2, which explains how establishing goals for yourself can help you to accomplish anything!

2

ESTABLISH GOALS

AND DON'T LET ANYTHING STOP YOU FROM REACHING THEM!

"A goal without a plan is just a wish."
~Quote credited to Antoine de Saint Exupéry

If you don't know your destination, you won't know how to get there. When you embark on a journey, you don't just start wandering aimlessly, do you? Usually, you choose your destination, determine the best route, and utilize a method of getting there (car, plane, train, boat, Hyperloop, etc.). The same concept applies to anything in life, especially when it comes to important things that you want to accomplish.

By setting a goal for yourself, you immediately have something to aim for. I recommend designing ambitious goals — things that you feel are just beyond your grasp — because it will motivate you to give that extra push to reach them. It is important to frame your goals in positive terms and with good feelings, affirming to yourself that you can reach them. Don't ever be afraid to dream big. Recall from Key 1: *If you believe in yourself, you can achieve anything.* ***BELIEVE IT AND ACHIEVE IT!***

It's been said that if your dreams don't scare you, they aren't big enough. Don't let fear be a deterrent; just think of it as the door between you and your reward on the other side. If you have the key to unlock the door, getting to the other side is easy, and this book is all about having the right Keys. Keep in mind: *fear is all in your head.* What you tell yourself is what you will believe. You must learn to ignore your doubts and fears, and I explain how to do that in Key 6.

When setting goals, it's best to establish a realistic time frame in which you hope to fulfill them. Committing to a deadline will help to motivate you and make it easier to manage your time and measure your progress. Likewise, you must plan from beginning to end, considering all possible obstacles or circumstances that may prevent a favorable outcome. By doing this, you will be better prepared to make revisions to your plan along the way. You won't be caught off-guard and paralyzed by a lack of options. In thinking far ahead, you are essentially guaranteeing a successful result.

Now, having told you that you must have specific goals which you strive for with passion, I am going to issue a disclaimer. Although you should always pursue your ambitions tenaciously, without giving up after the first (or second, or third) setback, you should also be aware that pushing too hard for something that's not meant to happen at that particular moment will not get you anywhere.

Have you heard the expression, "going against the grain"? You have to realize that when there's resistance, it's a sign that maybe you should back off a little. (I know, I know, make up my mind, right?!) All I'm saying is that not getting what you want when you want it doesn't mean that it's not right for you, or that you can't have it. It just means that perhaps it's not the right time. Haven't we all heard about couples who try desperately to have a baby and then, when they finally adopt, get pregnant?

Don't force any element of life, and don't go chasing things. If you are continually chasing after things, you'll find that you are always running. Instead, let things come to you. If you do the necessary groundwork and preparation through inspired action (I explain this in detail in Key 8), you will discover that what is meant for you will always find its way. Bear in mind that what you try to control ends up controlling you, so release your need to steer every movement. By freeing yourself, you are allowing things to take their natural course.

When you stop trying so hard to manipulate everything, all the doors will open for you. Just as the carefree dolphin rides the waves with ease and delight, so will the waves of your life carry you if you will just relax and let everything flow. Sometimes, when you try to force something to happen, the underlying fear of failure creates blocks and obstacles for you. As I said before, don't let fear deter you or prevent you from getting what you deserve.

To *CLEAR the FEAR*, you must *CLEAR your MIND*. Do this by meditating, doing yoga, taking time out in nature, connecting with friends, listening to music, dancing, taking a relaxing sea salt bath, or whatever it is that makes you happy. *Let go and let life flow*, and watch how quickly everything you desire comes to fruition. The best thing you can do is to get out of your own way and let your intuition guide you. Remember: **Resistance Prevents Results!**

There have been many times in my life that I didn't get exactly what I wanted because I was trying to control the situation, or I was resisting the natural flow of where my life was heading. But when I loosened my grip, what I ended up getting was so much better than I could have envisioned. For this I am grateful because I needed the time to learn more, gain experience, and mature into the situation. I needed to be ready to receive what was meant for me. Keep this in mind when establishing your goals: ***Relinquish to Receive!***

I realize that constructing plans to satisfy your grandest dreams can be frightening. What you are striving for will bring change, and change can be scary. Sometimes, just staying where you are is easier because where you are has become comfortable. But do you want to settle for the same boring, monotonous life, or do you want to live a life beyond your wildest dreams, feeling happier than you ever thought possible? By pushing yourself beyond your comfort zone, you will grow to become bigger and better than you could dare to imagine!

Setting and achieving goals is easier than you think — it simply requires *focus*. Focusing on what you want stimulates your brain's *Reticular Activating System* (RAS). The RAS is considered the brain's attention center. Its most significant function is to regulate the transition between sleep and wakefulness, but it is also responsible for responding to outside stimuli. It acts as a "filter" against all of the data we receive every day. It serves as a type of portal through which nearly all information enters our brain via our senses (except for smells, which go directly into the brain's emotional area).

We are bombarded by up to two million bits of data at any given moment. The brain can only process so much at a time, so your RAS "filter" sifts through the information and allows in what it thinks is important. But how does it know what is important? This is where *focus* comes in. Your brain determines what is most important by what you focus on *most*.

Obviously, the main objective — if you're trying to build a positive mindset — is to concentrate on the positive or good things in your life. By consciously thinking and talking about all of the things you appreciate and are grateful for, you are sending your subconscious mind a strong message via the RAS that there is so much more good than bad in your life. By bringing all of this good to the forefront of your reality, you are essentially creating your future happiness.

Have you ever noticed that people who say, "I'm not very confident," are not so self-assured? Or what about the people who say that they're always late? They seem to always be late. And people who complain that they can never lose weight … never lose weight! This is a type of scientific self-fulfilling prophecy.

Your Reticular Activating System tunes into what you focus on and tell yourself repeatedly. Then it processes that information, delivering it to your subconscious, which will provide you with evidence that what you're telling yourself is true. The more proof you see, the more you believe it is true, and the stronger your belief is, the more likely you are to keep telling yourself the same story. So it becomes a vicious circle of negative self-talk, proof, and belief. That is why you must break the cycle and learn to tell yourself positive things only. For example, don't say, "I suck at everything!" Instead, say "I succeed at everything!" Soon, your RAS will deliver proof that your new belief is true for you.

By reprogramming your Reticular Activating System to accept a positive belief system and deliver the corresponding good thoughts and visions to your subconscious mind, you are creating your intention for how you want your life to be. In effect, you are setting goals!

In order for your aspirations to materialize, you must structure a firm, detailed plan of what you want. In fact, when you devise goals for yourself, use strong, descriptive language for what you see as the end result. Don't *hope* or *wish for* or even *want* something to happen — rather, **intend** for it to happen. Know without a doubt that your objective will be met. Shaping your intent plays a vital role in prompting your subconscious into helping you realize your goal. It's a way for your conscious mind to connect with the subconscious, and for your RAS to stay focused on the desired outcome.

Here's a four-step method for reaching your goals:

1) Think of the goal that you would like to achieve. Focus on only one goal at a time. You can do this practice over

and over, but each time, select only one specific goal. If you have a really big goal, divide it up into smaller, more manageable pieces, so that you don't feel so overwhelmed by its magnitude. Each time one part of the goal is met, mark your achievement and reward yourself. This will signal to your brain to celebrate internally by releasing dopamine, thereby boosting your mood and motivating you to keep moving in the right direction.

2) Design your plan in definite terms of what you want. You must be very detailed here. Don't just say, "I want to lose weight." Say, "I *intend* on losing ten pounds in the next 60 days." Don't say, "I wish I could meet someone." Say "I *will* meet my dream partner in the next six months." By establishing definite expectations, your subconscious will go to work opening up ways for you to reach your goals, where before, you were just floating around, *hoping* for results.

3) Make an effort to feel what it would be like to reach your goal. (More on this in Key 4.) Really sense how happy you will be. Can you feel yourself smiling? Does this feeling

remind you of a time when you accomplished something great and you were happier than you ever thought you could be? Remember this; absorb the emotion and allow it to travel through your body. By re-enacting these good feelings, you are imprinting into your mind and body a reference point with which to reconnect.

4) Now that you know how great it will feel to achieve your goal, visualize the outcome as if it's happening now. (More on this subject in Key 9.) See where you are and notice the people around you. Are they congratulating you on your success? Are they marveling at your strength and determination? By acting as if your vision is a reality, you are tricking your subconscious mind into believing it is true. Once this happens, the rest of you will have no choice but to follow the direction of the script you've written in your mind.

You have the opportunity to write your own story — to create your own life. Why not make it good? Be positive and have only great expectations for your future. Visualize what you want, feel it with all your heart, and move forward toward your goal. You can't move forward if your mind is traveling in the opposite direction.

Achieving goals you've established for yourself is one of the most satisfying accomplishments you'll ever experience. The rewarding feeling you get translates into a sense of the utmost fulfillment. This raises the measure of your well-being and, therefore, your level of happiness — which is the primary goal. And really, who doesn't feel great when they get what they truly want? Ultimately, feeling great helps you to feel grateful, which just happens to be the next Key to happiness!

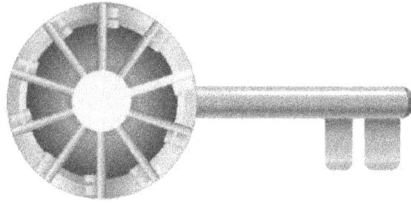

3

PRACTICE GRATITUDE
COUNT YOUR BLESSINGS

"If the only prayer you ever say in your entire life is 'Thank You,' it will be enough." ~Meister Eckhart

Being grateful is one of the quickest paths to happiness because it cultivates optimism. Every human being has the capacity to feel the emotion of gratitude, and we feel grateful when someone gives us something or does something nice for us. However, this type of gratefulness is often short-lived. It tends to disappear quickly, as the novelty of that new possession wears off or the memory of an act of kindness fades away.

To feel a more profound sense of happiness, you must make gratitude a state of mind and a way of life. To do this, you have to look at the big picture of life and realize that, overall, life is good. Of course there are ups and downs, but the only means of appreciating the goodness is to live through the not-so-good. The grateful person views all of life as a gift, even the bad aspects. After all, it is through our bad experiences that we learn and grow.

So how do you become grateful when you don't feel like there's much to be thankful for? Start with the basics. You're alive, right? Well, that's one huge thing to be grateful for. Begin to think of all of the positive things in your life and express your gratitude for them. For example, you could say: *"I am grateful to be alive. I feel immense gratitude for my family and friends. I am thankful for my home. I am grateful for the clothing I have and the shoes I wear. I am thankful to have clean, running water and food to eat."* When you observe the good things in your life, you automatically feel grateful.

In order to understand gratitude at its most basic level, we must first understand its opposite: ingratitude, which can also be described as thanklessness or ungratefulness. I would add to these terms one word: *resentment*, which is defined as "bitter indignation at having been treated unfairly." Often, we harbor resentment within us that prevents us from feeling gratitude. This resentment doesn't necessarily have to be felt toward a person or people who have wronged us; most times, people are resentful toward their situation. We often resent our lives and where we are within them.

Most people — especially in their young adult years — build a vision of their perfect life. They plan out their dreams and create an image of their own "happy ending." The problem with doing this is that most things in life don't transpire the way we envision they will, and everyone should be aware that nothing in life is perfect. Perfection doesn't exist, except in the dictionary. A good thing to keep in mind, though, is that sometimes things turn out better than we expect!

So, what happens when things in our lives don't unfold how we had hoped they would? We get angry and resentful that we didn't get what we wanted. Basically, we have a little temper tantrum. But think about what happens when toddlers have tantrums: usually, they cry and scream and throw themselves onto the ground, working themselves up into such a frenzy that they can't breathe, or talk, or think clearly.

Are you going to have a meltdown every time you don't get what you want in life? When people live their lives like this, they often act out a string of fits that lead from one to another, and the time in between is just a period of calming themselves down until the next outburst. So essentially, nothing ever gets accomplished except feeling continually upset over unfair circumstances.

But what is the solution? How do you get out of the vicious cycle of feeling resentment over how your life didn't pan out the way you had imagined it would, and then having angry outbursts to show your dissatisfaction? The answer: *forgiveness* and *gratitude*.

It is here again that we can learn a lot from children, who are experts in forgiveness and gratitude. They are quick to get over their tizzy fits and readily go back to being fast friends with someone they were just squabbling with. And have you noticed that children are in awe of everything around them? They take in their surroundings with amazement and wonder. Do you see the correlation here? Getting over something is basically releasing a grudge, which is a form of *forgiveness*; and being in awe of something is a form of *gratitude*.

Let's address forgiveness first. By forgiving anything you think is unfair or anyone you perceive as having committed wrongdoing against you, you are letting go of resentment. This is the first step in healing, which will lead to your ultimate happiness. Resentments can be deeply rooted and can last for years, so it is best to weed them out as soon as possible, or — better yet — prevent them altogether. Forgiveness is the solution for the first scenario, and gratitude for the latter.

If you are harboring long-standing anger or resentment toward something or someone, the way to eliminate it is to practice forgiveness. This is the easiest course to feeling happy and whole. The act of forgiving does not mean that you are absolving someone of their hurtful actions against you, and it does not indicate that you will forget what has happened. It is impossible to "unremember" events in our lives, and thank goodness — otherwise we wouldn't remember all of the good times we've experienced! But you also want to be able to recollect your negative experiences because you learned from these experiences: how to avoid dangerous situations, what not to do again, and whom not to trust. It's like having a scar — although the wound doesn't hurt anymore, the evidence of the injury is a badge of what you've endured and a reminder that you can heal from any pain in life. It's a symbol that you're a *SURVIVOR*!

So the key is not to *forget*, but to *forgive.* Forgiving means that you are no longer going to harbor the negative feelings that have been eating away at you; nor are you going to dwell upon the past and drag it into your future. Forgiving allows us to release the weight of our pain, while holding the valuable lessons from our past. Believe me, lifting that burden will not only *lighten your load*, but it will *enlighten your life*!

Forgiveness can also be shown to yourself. Often, we resent ourselves for not fulfilling our plans or living up to our own expectations. We can be our own harshest critics. But if you learn to forgive yourself and allow your life to unfold naturally, without being confined to a rigid plan, you will discover talents and abilities within yourself that you never knew of. Don't be set on just one path: there are many roads to one destination, and if you remain dead-set on just one, you may be destined to a path with a dead end!

As I mentioned before, gratitude is the best method to prevent resentment and feel contentment. Gratitude for what you have is the clearest route to happiness and to the true meaning of your life because it draws your attention to all of the good things around you. Being thankful prevents you from taking things for granted, by the mere fact that it brings about appreciation and awareness. If you take notice of even the smallest things, like a butterfly flitting around the garden, or hummingbirds zigzagging between the beautiful flowers, it will inspire a childlike awe within you. When you can be excited by the simple pleasures, you will recapture feelings of happiness for everyday things. This will bring you to the realization of what is genuinely important to you and allow you to identify what really matters. As a result, you will learn to give more of your time and attention to your priorities, thus bringing you more gratitude, appreciation, and, therefore, happiness. This happiness will cause you to feel even more grateful for what you have, creating a *Circle of Happiness*: *gratitude* → *appreciation* → *happiness.*

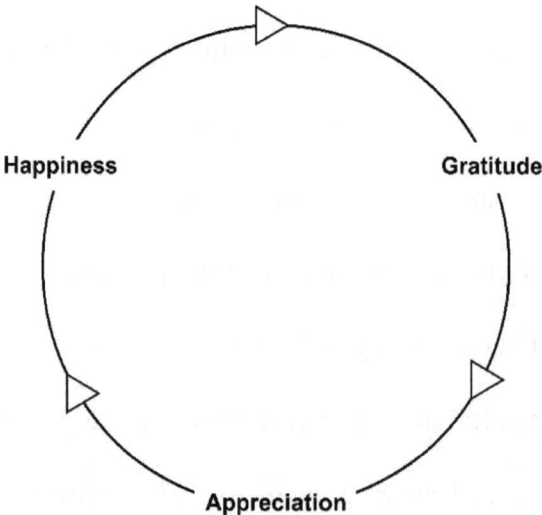

Happiness   **Gratitude**

Appreciation

If you want to live inside this circle of happiness, then I suggest that you live in gratitude. Dive in and make gratitude a part of your everyday life. Start by feeling grateful to be alive. Actively look for things to be thankful for, wherever you go. If you consciously utilize each of your senses to see, smell, hear, taste, and feel gratitude, you will create increased awareness and heightened perception, causing you to appreciate life that much more! Be grateful for every experience, and live every moment *in* the moment. (More on that in Key 5.)

When you are grateful, you are counting your blessings. When you feel blessed, you are in a state of bliss, or perfect happiness, which is a condition we all naturally strive for. As humans, happiness is our ultimate goal. Ask anyone what they want most in life, and the answer usually is: "To be happy." We are biologically designed to be happy, but our busy lives have us rushing around, ignoring our true nature and our essential needs. This is where practicing these Key techniques will help you to take back your happiness, and practicing gratitude might be the Master Key!

I recommend that you express thanks every night before you go to sleep. For example, you could say, *"I am grateful for this day and all that I have experienced and learned."* Just because you had a rough day doesn't mean you have to feel bad about it. Take the good and the bad out of every day and use what you assimilate to bring about a better tomorrow. Just as you say "thank you" every night, wake up every morning saying "thank you." One of my favorite sayings is, *"When I woke up this morning, I opened two gifts: my eyes."*

Each person is living a different experience, so wake up and be thankful for the uniquely positive things in *your* life. Create a good day by setting the tone and saying, *"I am grateful to wake up and embrace a new day. I am thankful for the opportunities that are waiting for me and for all of the things I will achieve."*

You can give thanks out loud or, even better, write down a few things every day that you're grateful for. A good daily practice is to make a list of **Three Good Things** about your day for which you are thankful. You can also keep a gratitude journal, in which you reflect on the moments in your day-to-day life when you've felt grateful. It helps to see things written out in your own handwriting because this makes you feel more connected. More importantly, studies have found that processing your emotions both verbally and in written form reduces activity in the amygdala, the fear center of the brain. By lowering your amygdala response, you diminish emotional distress, making you feel calmer and happier.

Another great idea is to start a gratitude jar or gratitude board for the whole family. Everyone can add gratitude notes daily, which can be read at the end of the week. Sentiments can be as simple as, "I'm grateful to spend time with my loved ones," or as silly as, "I'm thankful for my fuzzy slippers." You'll be pleasantly surprised to see how much your family appreciates what they have in their lives and how much there truly is to be grateful for!

Gratitude is associated with personal well-being. Grateful people are more optimistic, healthier (lower cholesterol, blood pressure, anxiety, and depression), and happier. When you're happy, it makes people around you feel happy, and vice versa. Happiness is contagious, and if you start a happiness movement, you'll set off a chain reaction that will spread quickly to everyone around you. Both happiness and unhappiness perpetuate themselves to the degree to which they are employed, so engage in happy thoughts and actions, and you'll shape an environment of optimism!

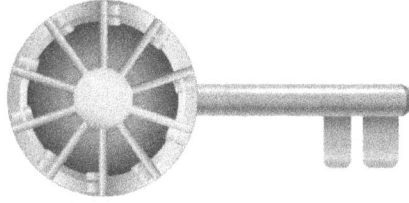

4

OBSERVE YOUR EMOTIONS

AND ADJUST ACCORDINGLY

"Emotion is stronger than any potion!" ~Nicco Boss

The way you *feel* is the best indicator of the type of emotional energy vibrating within you. Emotions manifest subjectively as strong feelings — happiness, sadness, anger, or fear — and are characterized by intense mental activity, accompanied by physiological and behavioral changes in the body. The physiology of emotion is closely connected to the arousal of the nervous system. The human nervous system is a network of cells called neurons and has two main parts: 1) the central nervous system (CNS), which consists of the brain and spinal cord; and 2) the peripheral nervous system (PNS), which consists of sensory neurons, ganglia (nerve cell clusters), and nerves that connect to one another and to the central nervous system.

Neurons are nerve cells that send and receive signals throughout the body. They communicate with each other by carrying impulses and transmitting information through an electrochemical process. They are responsible for sending, receiving, and interpreting information from all parts of the human anatomy. There are tens of billions of neurons in the body, and they are constantly creating electrochemical energy within us.

This energy, also referred to as bioelectromagnetism, or bioelectricity, consists of the electrical, magnetic, or electromagnetic fields produced by living organisms. Quantum physicists have discovered that our physical atoms are made up of vortices of vibrating energy, producing currents that create a vibrational frequency within us. Therefore, we are continually emitting vibrations relative to how we are feeling emotionally. When we are happy, we feel like we're floating because we're radiating on a higher frequency. When we're sad, or feeling down, it's because we're vibrating on a lower frequency.

Obviously, we can't always be upbeat, happy, and energetic. Life happens, and most of the time, it does not involve walking through a beautiful meadow wearing rose-colored glasses. Sometimes, in the midst of living our demanding lives, when we're *trying* to smell the roses, we just get pricked by the thorns and stung by the bees! All that does is make us wonder why we even bothered trying to be positive in the first place. But there is a reason for feeling pain and sadness and experiencing negative emotions. If we didn't know the difference between good and bad, or happy and sad, we wouldn't be able to decide what we sincerely want out of life.

By feeling sad, we know the contrast between that and the sense of happiness. This gives us a built-in gauge of how to measure our emotions, which is important, because it teaches us how to strive toward feeling good. When you feel good, you vibrate on a higher level, which has so many benefits. You are nicer to be around, you receive positive feedback from others, you get more accomplished, and your health is improved.

Just as feeling happy contributes to better overall health, better health generates feelings of greater happiness. The fastest course to comprehensive wellness is to sustain a healthy diet. Unhealthy eating habits can lead to depression, food addiction, and stress. A diet high in processed foods and refined carbohydrates, such as sugar and white starches will cause spikes in your blood sugar levels, followed by crashes, leaving you feeling tired, cranky, and depressed. Eating these foods may temporarily satisfy your taste buds and provide a quick boost of energy, but they won't help your mood. In addition, foods high in fat and sugar trigger the same pleasure centers in the brain that addictive drugs do, so the longer you maintain a junk-food diet, the harder it will be to break the bad habit.

To maintain good mental health and a positive outlook, it's crucial to develop and sustain good eating habits. Make sure you include plenty of protein, a colorful variety of fruits and vegetables, and lots of water. Protein (lean meat, fish, poultry, eggs, seafood, tofu, cheese, legumes, nuts and seeds) contains amino acids, which make up the chemicals your brain needs to regulate your thoughts and emotions. Adding protein to your meals can also slow the absorption of carbohydrates in your blood, controlling blood sugar levels and increasing the release of dopamine, which may elevate your mood and energy for several hours after consumption.

Fruits and vegetables are loaded with vitamins, minerals, and fiber, which keep us mentally and physically healthy. Vitamin D is a great mood-booster, and vitamins B-9 (folate) and B-12 may help ease depression. The fiber in fruits, vegetables, and other complex carbohydrates can slow the absorption of sugars into your bloodstream and increase serotonin, one of the "feel-good" chemicals. Lower blood sugar and higher serotonin levels have been found to decrease mood swings. Tryptophan helps the body to synthesize serotonin, and you might have heard that turkey contains a high level of that amino acid. In reality, all meats contain tryptophan — turkey more than chicken, but not as much as pork. It is possible to help your body synthesize serotonin by eating meat protein combined with complex carbs. But if you're a vegan, foods such as whole grains, nuts and seeds, legumes, dark leafy greens, mushrooms, and healthy carbs such as fruits and potatoes will do the trick.

There's definitely a link between your diet and your emotions. Protein, carbohydrates, vitamins, and minerals affect your metabolism, hormones, and neurotransmitters, which are mood chemicals produced in the brain. Dopamine, another one of the feel-good neurotransmitters, can be increased by eating a diet which includes: sufficient, yet balanced, portions of dairy foods like milk, yogurt, and cheese; unprocessed meats such as chicken, turkey, and beef; omega-3-rich fish like salmon, mackerel, and sardines; eggs; fruits and vegetables; nuts and seeds such as walnuts, almonds, chia and flax seeds; and dark chocolate!

The cycle of good health and happiness starts with a healthy diet, and it doesn't matter where the cycle starts; it's important to take the first step and to keep going! So if you can't seem to just "get happy" for no reason, make *one* small change in your diet and gradually build up to creating good habits. Cut down or eliminate something from your diet that you know is really not good for you. Try substituting that with a healthier option. If you do this gradually and stick to it, you'll find that you can really develop healthy eating habits, and soon you won't miss that junk food because your body will naturally extinguish the craving for it. It's true that food can change your mood!

Besides adopting healthy eating habits and focusing on maintaining a positive mindset, three other components that are crucial to lifting your emotions are: 1) *Sleep*, 2) *Exercise*, and 3) *Achievement*. Paying particular attention to these three pillars in your life will lead to greater emotional fulfillment and, as a result, maximized happiness. *So stop drowning in an ocean of negative emotion and start swimming in a **SEA** of glee!*

One of the most important building blocks to happiness is making sure to get plenty of *Sleep* because it provides your body with the rest and recovery from all of the stresses of your day. Chronic lack of sleep is linked to anxiety and depression, as well as other illnesses. During a full sleep cycle, the body heals itself by releasing hormones that repair cells and form tissue, which strengthen the immune system to fight disease. It is also the only time the brain can clean itself of toxins.

Recently, neuroscientists at the University of Rochester Medical Center discovered a previously unrecognized cleansing system that flushes wastes from the brain. This highly organized system was dubbed the "glymphatic system," since it acts much like the body's lymphatic system. It is best described as a network of pipes or tubes attached to the brain's blood vessels, and its purpose is to drain away waste products that have accumulated during the wakeful hours of the day. The glymphatic system is only highly active during deep sleep, which highlights the necessity of getting a good night's rest. Waste clearance is of critical importance to every organ of the body, including the brain, whose glial cells wash away the toxins responsible for Alzheimer's disease and other neurological disorders.

Thanks to modern technological advances, neuroscientists are discovering more about the brain and its functions. The glymphatic system operates only in a living brain, and scientists were able to study it using new imaging technology called two-photon microscopy. They injected fluorescent tracer into the cerebrospinal fluid of mice (whose brains are incredibly similar to humans) and were able to track the path of the fluid whooshing through the sleeping brain and eliminating toxins. Observation of the cleansing process revealed the removal of beta-amyloid (the protein known to accumulate in the brains of patients with Alzheimer's disease), and completion of the cycle was verified as the toxic waste was delivered to the liver to be expelled.

Another fascinating finding of the study was that, during sleep, the brain's cells shrink in size, creating wider pathways to allow for more efficient waste removal. This indicates yet another essential reason that a sufficient amount of regular, non-interrupted, restful sleep is vital to brain function and health. The brain has two different functional states: when we are awake and conscious of our surroundings, and when we are asleep. When we are awake, our brain cells are working very hard at processing information, but when we are asleep, our brains work just as hard at getting rid of all of the waste that has built up throughout the day. A clean mind is a healthy mind, which promotes a healthy body. When mind and body are unified in health, we are complete.

Mind and body unity can also be achieved through regular *Exercise*. In our hectic lives, it can be difficult to find time to work out, and even when we have the time, we're often just too tired to lift a finger. Unless your livelihood is dependent upon staying fit, physical training can be a real chore. However, it is important to make time to do some light aerobic exercise. As little as thirty minutes, three times a week will benefit your health immensely and the endorphins released will provide a flood of positive feelings into your system.

The last of the three pillars of emotional health is *Achievement*, which is a strong driving force behind most people's actions. Accomplishing what we aspire to do provides a deep sense of purpose in life and creates pure emotional fulfillment. One of the strongest needs we have as human beings is the desire to feel important; everyone craves recognition and appreciation. We all want to feel as if we bring something unique to this world and we are gratified when we are recognized as being special and significant. Finding happiness through achievement is a major premise of this book: we learn, visualize, take action, stay positive, ignore our doubts and fears, observe our emotions, strive to live in the present moment, and stay grateful while we set our goals — all to achieve what we believe.

Positive emotions don't just bring fleeting happiness. Practicing gratitude and focusing on maintaining positive emotions have real and lasting benefits. Studies in the *Science of Happiness* have revealed that positive emotions expand our minds and our hearts in such a way that we are able to see the big picture. Positive emotions widen the scope of what we see and heighten our awareness of opportunities. When you are in a positive state of mind, you see more possibilities because you are open to them. People who are more positive tend to be more successful.

Additionally, if you are able to increase and maintain positive emotions over a relatively short period of time, you will actually effect change on a cellular level. Scientists have estimated that, on average, across all body systems, people replace 1% of their cells each day. This equates to 30% cellular replacement in one month and 100% in one season. I guess it's no coincidence that it takes about three months to learn a new habit or make a lifestyle change. Isn't it exciting to know that, in as little as three months, you can turn over all of your cells and transform your old, negative self into a whole new, stronger, better, and more positive individual? By increasing your daily diet of positive emotions, you can literally change who you are!

But maintaining positive emotions one hundred percent of the time is not the way to sustained gratification, nor is it realistic. A variety of emotions is far more beneficial to a person's overall well-being. This diversity of emotions, called *emodiversity*, includes happiness, gratitude, contentment, hope, and love, as well as sadness, fear, anger, contempt, and anxiety. It's okay — and actually healthy — to feel them all. In fact, crying is recommended when you're upset because it activates the parasympathetic nervous system, releases natural opioids in the brain (subduing pain), stimulates oxytocin production, and flushes toxins from your body.

It's perfectly normal and acceptable to feel angry if you're wronged or sad when dealing with loss. Trying to be happy when you really aren't will only make you feel worse. Suppressing a negative feeling simply allows it to grow internally, which only helps to feed the beast, rather than slay it. Worse yet, if left unchecked, consistent forced positivity becomes extremely harmful because false-positive thoughts that your subconscious mind doesn't legitimately accept as truth have the potential to manifest externally as illness.

By recognizing and expressing all of our emotions, we are able to apply the appropriate action to diffuse negative feelings. We must allow ourselves to release the negativity as a method to decompress (just letting it all out), and learn to replace the negative emotions with positive ones at the appropriate time. Begin by asking yourself why you feel the way you do. When you have more clarity about the *why*, it's much easier to address *how* to resolve the issue and move forward to a better place.

It's important to keep in mind that, just as negative emotions aren't unhealthy in every case, stress is not always detrimental. Stress is a natural physical and mental reaction that helps us cope with adversity in life. We are evolutionarily designed to use stress as a means of survival. We can consider this type of stress "good stress." When we are under threat, our sympathetic nervous system triggers our "fight or flight" response, causing the adrenal glands to release the hormone cortisol. However, the stress response is meant to be quick: deal with the problem at hand — utilizing the dose of cortisol your body just equipped you with to either fight or flee — and then get back to normal. But if you are under constant stress, your body will continually release cortisol into your system, building up dangerous levels in your blood. This is what is considered "bad stress." Long-term stress is harmful to your health in so many ways: it can lead to poor sleep and insomnia, weaken the immune system, interfere with learning and memory, cause weight gain and high blood pressure, and increase the risk for anxiety, depression, heart disease, and mental illness.

A direct counter to the emergency reflex of the sympathetic nervous system is the calming response of the parasympathetic nervous system. When this system is activated, heart and breathing rates slow down, sweating ceases, and digestion resumes. That's why it's often referred to as the "rest and digest" or "tend and befriend" system. As I stated in Key 1, the main component of the parasympathetic nervous system is the vagus nerve, and stimulating it triggers the release of the chemical messenger acetylcholine, which is the most abundant of the approximately 100 neurotransmitters that have been identified thus far. Not only does acetylcholine initiate muscle action — including relaxing the heart muscles and, thus, slowing heart rate — but it is also associated with memory, learning, motivation, and attention.

Activity in the vagus nerve, known as the "caretaking nerve," is strongly related to feelings of connection and care toward others, which fosters empathy and compassion for others, as well as for oneself. Scientific research provides evidence that healthy vagal tone is linked to positive emotions, resulting in physical, psychological, and emotional well-being. Low vagal tone, on the other hand, is correlated with inflammation, heart problems, negative moods, and depression.

Studies reveal the interconnectedness between the brain and the rest of the body and indicate that about 80% of vagal nerve fibers are dedicated to sending signals to the brain regarding the state of the peripheral body. Recently, scientists at ETH Zürich in Switzerland identified how "gut instincts," specifically those associated with anxiety and fear, are conveyed to the brain via the vagus nerve. These instincts, or emotional intuitions, literally travel up the vagus nerve to the brain to warn of impending danger. The brain then relays messages back down to the body with instructions of how to react in the situation. Healthy communication along the mind-body feedback loop between the brain and the gut will regulate mood and moderate certain types of fear and anxiety. The types of signals sent make the difference in whether the sympathetic or parasympathetic nervous systems are activated.

The bi-directional communication between the central nervous system (CNS) and viscera (gut) is referred to as the "gut-brain axis" and is critical to modulating, or regulating, mood and affect. Both innate anxiety and learned fear are linked to vagus nerve signals traveling via limbic neurotransmitter systems. The *Limbic System* consists of several relatively small portions of the brain including — but not limited to — the hippocampus, hypothalamus, amygdala, thalamus, and cingulate cortex. Although the limbic system is responsible for many processes, such as hormone production, memory function, and autonomic nervous system regulation, its primary role is controlling emotions and governing emotional behavior.

Hyperactivity in the limbic brain areas have been associated with affective disorders like depression and bipolar disorder. Habitually living in a state of fear, panic, or worry will induce a hyperactive limbic system response, which only feeds anxiety and perpetuates the problem. Vagus nerve stimulation has been linked to diminished adverse activity in the limbic system, thereby reducing the manifestation of illnesses and disorders, and improving cognitive brain function like memory and alertness, as well as emotional responses to environmental factors.

Emotion is stronger than any potion, and keeping it positive is a major step toward serenity. By quelling the vagus nerve response to imagined anxiety and fear, you are sending messages along your mind-body feedback loop, signaling to your organs to produce an inner calm by activating your parasympathetic (rest and digest) nervous system. I cannot emphasize enough how essential it is to build mind-body synergy in order to create inner balance and ***STRESS LESS***. But how?

R-E-L-A-X!

- *R*eflect and practice gratitude because appreciation elevates optimism and leads to better physical and psychological health.

- *E*xercise regularly: Twenty to thirty minutes of light aerobic activity releases endorphins and will consume excess cortisol in your system.

- *L*augh! Laughter lowers stress hormone levels. If you feel that you have nothing to laugh about, smile. Even a fake smile can trigger happiness because the act of smiling is recognized by your brain, activating a release of endorphins.

- *A*pply deep-breathing techniques and meditation practice in your daily life. Deep breathing stimulates the body's naturally-calming parasympathetic nervous system, and meditation generates emotional balance. Mindfulness meditation, in particular, promotes measurable growth in the brain regions involved in learning, memory, and emotion. (More on mindfulness in Key 5.)

- *X*-Variable: You fill in the blank and do *X* — whatever makes you happy. Maybe you like to listen to music, or dance, or go out into nature. Perhaps socializing with your friends de-stresses you, or maybe just allowing yourself some quiet time alone works for you. Also know that this can change from day-to-day and week-to-week. Just do something that brings joy to your life.

Relaxing allows you to delve into your inner world to find the sanctuary of the present time. It is there that you will release your stresses and lift your limitations. In the realm of relaxation, you will encounter the space that houses your subconscious mind, which is the doorway to the answers and the strength that you are seeking. Your subconscious will allow you to make a shift in your consciousness and will give you the chance to release the emotional baggage of your past.

Emotions can be positive or negative, and each has a consequence. The good news is that, by choosing how you allow yourself to feel, you determine the quality of your life. Emotion is indeed stronger than any potion because it has the power to create your experience. Don't allow emotion to cause a commotion; rather, make it the key to your jollity. Think of emotion as the *key*-motion to your well-being, and you will never again use that key to open any door but the one to your happiness!

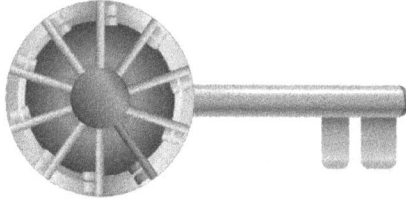

5

STAY IN THE PRESENT

BE HERE NOW

"If you are depressed, you are living in the past. If you are anxious, you are living in the future. But if you are at peace, you are living in the present."
~Lao Tzu

If you want to be genuinely happy, you must live in the present moment. Right now is really all you ever have. Even when you think about the past, you're doing it *now*; and when you worry about the future, you're experiencing that feeling *now*. The moment that we call *NOW* is appropriately called the present because it truly is a gift that we receive every second that we are alive.

Life happens quickly, and the dynamics of your life can change your experience and perception of it in an instant. What made you happy ten, five, or even one year ago most likely won't bring you joy today, just as what makes you happy today won't necessarily bring you contentment in the future. This is especially true if your happiness depends on outside means. If you attribute your happiness to external sources that you have no control over or that may easily disappear, you will always live in turmoil over the threat of something taking your happiness away.

Happiness comes from tapping into yourself and finding the gift inside — the present. Consider it this way: you and the present moment are *inside* sources of happiness; and other people, the past, and the future are *outside* sources. So look within and you will win! Of course you can derive joy from cherished memories of the past or from hopes for the future, but don't dwell there. True bliss comes from what you can't long for or miss, and you can't miss what you have right now!

If you live your life in regret over what happened in the past or blame yourself for the mistakes you made when you were young, or especially if you ruminate in sadness over the "good old days" and how much better things used to be, you will lead yourself right into depression. You can never get that time back, so wasting precious moments mourning those past times just steals away the only thing you really have in life — the present.

Sadness, anger, regret, and resentment (in particular) are all emotions that — if left unchecked — become toxic and even deadly. As I described in Key 3, resentment is defined as "bitter indignation at having been treated unfairly." It is also "persistent ill will at something regarded as a wrong, insult, or injury." Let's break down the word: the Latin *re-* means again (and again), indicating repetition; *sent* comes from the Latin *sentient*, meaning "feeling." Thus, when you harbor resentment, you are *re-feeling* sadness, regret, and anger over something that happened in the past.

You must let go of the past and dissolve any and all resentment you hold against anyone who has hurt you; and you must get over events and/or circumstances that you feel impacted your life negatively. As I explained in Key 3, you do this by forgiving.

When you are depressed about the past, you are grieving over the fact that things didn't work out how you wanted them to, or feeling sadness over the loss of the way things used to be. Forgiving allows you to let go and release your resentment. It means giving up all hope for a better past. Think about it: you can't change the past (unless you find a method of traveling back in time), so by dwelling on it, you are creating unnecessary depression by living in a moment that only exists in your imagination. By continuing to insist that your past should somehow change (coulda/shoulda/woulda), you are dooming yourself to endless blame and suffering. Unless and until you stop living in the past, you will perpetuate a life of misery. And no one wants to be miserable. So start on the path to forgiveness now!

Forgiveness is powerful! Forgiving others who have caused you harm will actually reduce your stress and foster happiness. Try it right now. Think about someone who has really hurt you, whom you haven't forgiven. Do you think they feel your resentment and are harmed by it? No. You're only harming yourself by letting your resentment eat away at you. So put an end to it immediately! Think about the transgression and forgive them for what they did. The first and most important step is to say out loud to yourself: "(*Their name*), I forgive you for (*what they did to hurt you*)." The next step is to express your forgiveness to the offender in person, by phone, or in writing. If you want/need to avoid contact with the person, or if they are no longer alive, practicing this task alone is just as healing. Simply write down on paper what you would have said to them in person. Then dispose of the paper — either by throwing it away or by burning it — as a means of eliminating your attachment to the incident once and for all.

By accepting that the transgression occurred and being willing to forgive the offender, you are confronting the issue and releasing your urge to punish or seek vengeance upon them. This will increase your compassion toward that person for their own suffering and misguided intentions, which will allow you to fully let go and start to heal.

An important point to bear in mind is that forgiveness *DOES NOT* mean that you condone the offense or absolve the offender of responsibility for his or her wrongdoing. It also *DOES NOT* mean you will forget what has happened. Offering forgiveness does not signify that you are weak or foolish. In fact, it shows that you are strong enough to let go, which often requires more strength than to hold on.

Forgiveness *DOES* mean that you are breaking free from the hurt, anger, and resentment you've suffered, thereby releasing that person's authority over your emotional well-being. Forgiveness is the acceptance you feel and the openness and freedom of moving forward. By accepting and forgiving what has happened, you are giving the next moment a chance. You are no longer renting space in your mind to the past, but instead allowing the present to move in.

Don't forget to forgive yourself too. We often blame ourselves for the mistakes we made in the past that we feel ruined our lives or prevented us from having the life we really wanted. We say to ourselves, "If only I had done this differently," or "If only I hadn't screwed that up…." What you must realize is that each decision you made in the past has led you to the present moment, and that's all you have. Our mistakes make us stronger and wiser. They teach us what *not* to do again, and that's the greatest lesson of all. Could you imagine if we didn't learn from our errors? We'd be doomed to living in a perpetual cycle of mistake-making, making our whole life one big mistake!

Just as regretting the past does not benefit you, fretting over the future will not serve you. When you worry over what *may* occur in the future, you are creating anxiety in your life over something that most likely will never happen. Just as the past no *longer* exists, the future does not exist *yet* — and it never will! At each moment that we arrive into our future, it becomes our present; therefore, the future never exists. And as we live in each present moment, the future we envisioned turns out to be nothing like the present that we are actually living.

Worrying about how your future will unfold and trying to predict every detail is indeed a waste of the present time. I'm not suggesting that you live your life recklessly, abandoning all plans due to a lack of your control over what is going to happen. Of course we must live our lives setting goals, making plans, and exercising precautions in case something happens — that's the reason we buy insurance. Thankfully, we rarely need to use it. But when we do, we're glad we have it. Think about it like this: we don't go around carrying an umbrella with us every day wherever we go. We buy umbrellas and keep them handy *in case* we need them. When we know there's a good chance that it will rain, we take them along. Sometimes we forget to bring them, and the worst that happens is, we get wet! The whole point is, worrying is like a rocking chair — it gives you something to do, but it doesn't get you anywhere. If you give all of your thoughts to worrying about tomorrow, tomorrow will steal away your today.

One of my favorite stories that really puts into perspective the advantage of living in the moment is "The Farmer's Fortune":

Once upon a time, there was an old farmer who had worked his crops for many years. One day his horse ran away. Upon hearing this news, his neighbors came to visit. "Such bad luck," they said, sympathetically.

"Perhaps," the farmer replied.

The next morning, the horse returned, bringing with it three other wild horses. "What great luck!" the neighbors exclaimed.

"Perhaps," replied the old man.

The following day, his son tried to ride one of the untamed horses, was thrown, and broke his leg. The neighbors again came to offer their sympathy on his misfortune.

"Perhaps," answered the farmer.

The day after, military officials came to the village to draft young men into the army. Seeing that the son's leg was broken, they passed him by. The neighbors congratulated the farmer on how well things had turned out.

"Perhaps," said the farmer.

This story exhibits the power of living in the present and not worrying about the future or dwelling on the past. The farmer took things day by day and didn't let the events of his life affect his thinking or his perspective on things. Had he worried about his horse running away, or regretted his son's injury, it would have been time and emotions wasted because, as you read, those events worked out for the best. He changed his ***mishaps*** into ***perhaps***!

There are often times in our lives when what we first perceive as a curse ends up to be a blessing. Sometimes an unfulfilled wish can result in being the best thing that could have happened. Remain cautiously optimistic, or "positively expectant," and know that fortune will always follow misfortune. There's a reason for expressions like: "Without the rain, there would be no rainbows;" and "Stars can't shine without darkness." Remember this:

REJECTION *turns into*

REDIRECTION,

CORRECTION,

and eventually

CONNECTION!

Being connected to the present moment brings you happiness because it makes you realize what you have *right now*. This is called mindfulness and can be practiced in so many ways. Examples include mindful breathing, mindful yoga, and mindfulness meditation, which allows you to focus on your breath and pay attention to thoughts and sensations without judgement. Research has demonstrated that mindfulness meditation increases gray matter in five areas of the brain, including the left prefrontal cortex (responsible for calm, optimism, and happiness) and the hippocampus (the region involved in memory, learning, and emotional control).

Mindfulness meditation also reduces symptoms of anxiety, depression, and chronic pain. One famous study conducted under the Mindfulness-Based Stress Reduction (MBSR) program at the University of Massachusetts Medical Center examined patients suffering from chronic pain. After practicing mindfulness meditation for several weeks, a majority of the participants reported a reduction in pain of up to 50% of their original level! This outcome asserted that "mindfulness facilitates an uncoupling of the sensory dimension of the pain experience." Simply stated, learning to be in the present moment through mindfulness practices effectively "turns off" the alarm response to pain, thereby reducing suffering.

If you learn to fully engage in the present and truly live consciously for each moment, everything becomes better and bolder — the colors you see, the scents you smell, the sounds you hear, the textures you feel, and even the food you taste. Try this exercise: the next time you eat, really immerse yourself in the experience. Consciously think about what you are consuming. First, consider what had to happen for you to have the food you are about to enjoy. Think of the conditions that were needed to grow the food you are eating; the sun, the rain, and the soil had to be just right to produce the sustenance you sometimes take for granted. How many people toiled to harvest the grains, fruits, vegetables, etc. that are nourishing you? Who prepared the food you are so fortunate to be enjoying?

Before you indulge in the first bite of your food, take a good look at it — remember, we eat with our eyes first. Next, smell its delicious aroma because the sense of smell amplifies the sense of taste. Then, with each bite you take, don't just devour your food. Chew it slowly, taste it, let it roll around on your tongue and really sink into your taste buds. When you do this, you genuinely appreciate the flavors of your food. They become much deeper and more intense, and your meal becomes a celebration for your senses. When you savor your food and make eating a multi-sensory experience, your brain releases endorphins and other feel-good chemicals, such as dopamine and serotonin. This simple exercise of relishing the moment in gratitude for your food will provide countless benefits and immeasurable happiness! (Bonus side benefit: eat slowly = eat less = lose weight!)

An endeavor similar to savoring your food is that of exercising a ***Mindful Minute*** every day. This is an important practice which incorporates almost all of the Keys. Even if your days are so hectic that you can't find just five minutes to meditate, everyone has *one* minute every day to spend practicing mindfulness. Being mindful develops awareness of the present moment and allows us to accept experiences without judging them. So if you take only one element from this entire book, make it the *Mindful Minute*.

Set a timer for sixty seconds and, in that minute, focus on *NOW*. Repeat the word, "Now…now…now." Or you can say, "I am here now;" or "All I have is now." Remember to breathe in deeply and exhale fully for the entire minute. This short and easy activity will help you to stop the world;

surprisingly, this brief amount of time can help you reset your focus and your outlook. I guarantee that spending one *Mindful Minute* every day will calm you enough to feel like you can take on anything. I'd even venture to bet that soon, you'll be adding more *Mindful Minutes* throughout your day (and feeling better with each passing one).

Taking three *Mindful Minutes* a day is yet more beneficial. A really good habit to develop is to merge your *Mindful Minutes* with your **Three Good Things** gratitude practice (Key 3). Set an alarm for three separate times daily, spread out throughout the day (good times are around breakfast, lunch, and dinner), during which you can take a minute to practice mindfulness, and after which you can write down something you're grateful for. By combining these two exercises (three, if you incorporate **Savor Your Food**), you are fortifying the impact they have and creating within yourself a much greater sense of gratitude, reward, and fulfillment. Neuroscientific studies show that short practices sprinkled throughout the day can be a powerful way to promote neuroplasticity and lasting change in the brain.

Another suggestion is to take a *Mindful Minute* each time you encounter something challenging in your day. For instance, we've all had the experience of dealing with lagging computers or slow Wi-Fi when we need to get work done. Rather than getting frustrated and pulling out your hair, use the time as a perfect opportunity to take a *Mindful Minute*. It will instantly calm you down, and chances are, by the time the minute is over, your network will be back up to speed and running once again. Waiting at a red light is also an excellent time to incorporate this exercise. By pausing for a *Mindful Minute* to relax and reflect on things for which you are grateful, you are taking the fastest route to the intersection of the *present moment* and *genuine happiness*.

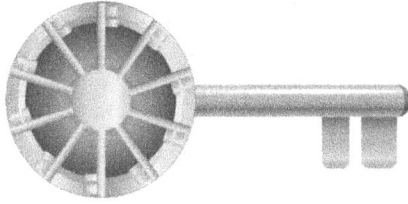

6

IGNORE YOUR DOUBTS AND FEARS
DON'T GIVE IN TO NEGATIVE SELF-TALK

"Your mind is a garden, your thoughts are the seeds.
You can grow flowers, or you can grow weeds."
~Unknown

What you feed will grow, so whatever you do, don't feed your fears. What you focus on tends to become greater, so it's best to give all of your attention to the positive aspects of your life. Not every day is good, but there is something good in every day, no matter how little it may be. Make a conscious effort to see the good things, and you will soon find so many more good things to appreciate. We all have a choice to see the positive in a situation, or to see the negative. Feed your positive thoughts and you will reap the rewards.

A short but powerful parable about the Two Wolves describes this concept very well:

An old Cherokee Chief was teaching his grandson about life....

"A fight is going on inside me," he said to the boy. "It is a terrible fight and it is between two wolves.

"One is evil — he is anger, envy, sorrow, regret, greed, arrogance, self-pity, guilt, resentment, inferiority, lies, false pride, superiority, self-doubt, and ego.

"The other is good — he is joy, peace, love, hope, serenity, humility, kindness, benevolence, empathy, generosity, truth, compassion, and faith.

"This same fight is going on inside you, and inside every other person, too."

The grandson thought about it for a minute and then asked his grandfather, "Which wolf will win?"

The old Chief simply replied, "The one you feed."

This story is an old one, but it resonates so much because it's true. If you constantly feed your fears and doubts, they will multiply like weeds. But if you nourish your mind with happy, hopeful thoughts, you will perpetuate a way of thinking that is positive.

You may be thinking that you can't just ignore your doubts and fears. They're there. They're a part of you, and the more you try to ignore them, the more you think about them. The more you think about them, the more you validate them, and the more fearful you grow. It becomes a vicious cycle. The key is to focus on something you appreciate.

Appreciation, which is a form of gratitude, is a fundamental tool for obtaining happiness. Research shows that it is physiologically impossible to be in a state of appreciation and in a state of fear at the same time. By thinking about things you appreciate, you block your doubts and fears. Appreciation nurtures optimism, and optimism cultivates happiness. So instead of being on a negative, downward spiral, you position yourself on a positive, uplifting track. Once you get into the habit of feeding your mind positive, happy thoughts, you will train it to accept those thinking patterns more readily, helping it to automatically filter out negative thoughts.

We all have the capacity to think positively, but all too often we give in to negative thoughts and ideas because it's what we're used to, and we fall back into our comfort zone. If we're faced with anything unknown or something that we don't understand, we tell ourselves we can't do it: "I'm not good enough, so why even try?" Sound familiar?

This is an example of fear-based thinking. Most times, doubts and fears stem from years or even decades of negative programming. Unfortunately, many people grow up being told that they'll never accomplish certain things, due to physical constraints, for example, or because of limitations on their intelligence or financial standing. Often, the criticisms people hear about themselves become the value system by which they perceive themselves and interpret their abilities.

This belief system effectively becomes a blueprint of how you live your life: the choices you make, the risks you take, and the successes you celebrate. Your "mind-limiting talk" will unfortunately create your self-image, which determines your actions, your behavior, and even your abilities. Essentially, you are creating your own shortcomings according to your thoughts and expectations.

We have all been molded by statements and sayings from our parents, our friends, society, etc., creating our restricting beliefs. If you're a female, you might believe you're not good at math and science; or if you look different from other people, you might think that nobody will like you; or maybe you feel like you'll never prosper in the business world due to a lack of education; or that you won't triumph at sports because you don't have the "right body;" or that it's impossible to succeed in marriage because "everyone gets divorced." When convictions are so deeply ingrained in your brain, it's hard to release them. But there is a way! It is possible to change your thinking patterns, alter your behavior, and transform your life.

It was previously thought that, after childhood growth and development, the brain was permanently fixed. However, thanks to modern neuroscientific research, we now know that this is not true. Our brains are capable of changing until the day we die. This is really great news because it means that all of those thought patterns and beliefs that were seemingly hardwired into our brains from childhood can be reprogrammed. All of the false ideologies we've subscribed to, as well as the outdated societal paradigms that we've learned to accept, no longer have to control the way we think, what we believe, and how we live our lives!

But what makes this possible? The answer is *neuroplasticity*: the brain's ability to reorganize itself and change its physical structure and function by forming new neural connections throughout life. The neural synapses and pathways are altered based on input from experiences, emotions, behaviors, habits, and even thoughts. So, whether you have good or bad habits, or if you have positive or negative patterns of thinking, your brain will forge neural imprints accordingly. The more you practice your mode of thinking, the deeper these impressions become, creating deeply-entrenched value systems. Think of it as treading on grass: the more you walk along the same area, the more defined the path becomes. So the objective is to improve your life by changing your thoughts to good ones and, therefore, building a better brain and creating permanent good habits.

Breaking habits can be very difficult to do, and it takes time — but it can be done. Even if you don't necessarily feel positive or happy, if you begin to think happy thoughts and say positive things, you will engineer neural channels in your brain that shape a positive thought process. Positive thinking is a learned ability, and the more you practice it, the easier it becomes as you strengthen the neural pathways of your brain and collect cellular memory to take you there again. It won't happen overnight, but it will occur if you are consistent and persistent. I described in Key 4 that we replace 1% of our cells each day and 100% in one season. Similarly, it takes several weeks to a few months to develop new habits. So give it a chance to take effect. Like working out to keep your body fit, you must also exercise your brain to make it as healthy as possible.

Meditation is an ideal method to tap into your brain power and remove yourself from negative thinking because, essentially, you're not thinking! You're concentrating on your breathing and not focusing on worries, troubles, and fears. Another helpful process of structuring a positive mindset is saying affirmations. I know it can feel funny to say things like: *"I love and accept myself for who I am. Today, I abandon my old habits and take up new, more positive ones. I am the* architect of my life, and I will design the best life possible! I possess the talents and qualities to be successful. I have choices in life, and I choose happiness." Once you get used to making these statements, they're like little pep-talks. They really work wonders to make you feel great about who you are and what you have to offer! The biggest benefit is, your subconscious is listening, and with each positive statement, your brain is creating a new, happy pathway to form a positive opinion about yourself.

An excellent strategy to remove self-doubt is to pay attention to your strengths. Do more of what you're good at and what you enjoy. The happiest people are those who recognize their strengths and put them into practical use. The most accomplished people take what they are good at and apply it to create a rewarding career. If you still don't think that you have any redeeming qualities, here's a fun fact: every person can do at least one thing better than ten thousand other people. So start searching for your "one thing," and I guarantee you'll find countless things you're good at that will make the world a better place!

In Key 1 I told you, "The quickest way to lose your identity is to compare yourself to others." First of all, if you're trying to be like someone else, then you're not being true to yourself. It's okay to find inspiration in others, and emulating someone successful by adopting their work ethic or positive outlook or desire to do good for others is perfectly fine, as long as you remember to put your own personality into whatever you do. Always concentrate on yourself, your abilities, and your strengths. You are who you are. You cannot change that and become someone else. Embrace your uniqueness because, once you do, you will be free to become the best *you* possible!

When you look to see what others are doing, it takes away precious time from your own life. If you're wasting your time analyzing other people's lives, then you're building a state of anxiety within yourself because you're trying to see if you measure up. When you worry about if and how you're going to fit in — whether that be socially, physically, or financially —

you take away from your life in the present moment. Essentially, you're living in a fictitious future. If you fear what *may* happen tomorrow, you're sabotaging your chance for happiness because you're establishing false, negatively-charged scenarios in your mind about how your life will unfold.

You become so worried about how someone might perceive you or what they may say about you, that you lose sight of who you are and what you have to offer *now*! All I can say to that is, if people are going to talk about you, you can't stop them; and if they're so busy worrying about you, obviously they're not happy with their own lives. If that's the case, then you don't want to associate with them anyway. They'll only bring you down with their negativity and low vibrational frequency, and the whole point of what you're trying to do is to become more positive in your life. If people don't like or accept you, that's their problem. If you feel insecure about what people think, a good quote to live by that has stood the test of time is, "Be who you are and say what you feel, because those who mind don't matter and those who matter don't mind."

Sometimes, the only way to dispel beliefs and conquer fears is by facing them head-on. Recognize the fear, acknowledge it, and then release it. By recognizing the fear, you are able to accept that it exists. Once you accept something, you are capable of moving forward in addressing what needs to be done to eliminate it — namely, appreciating everything good and positive in your life. By accepting a problem, you are enabling yourself to find the solution, and by inviting good thoughts, you are releasing the bad. Have confidence that you can accomplish anything you set your mind to. When your mind is made up, fears disappear. That's why it is so important to have goals — they give you something to strive for, which offers hope and erases fear.

A really great tool to use in feeding your positivity is to smile often, even if you don't feel like it. Smiling affects your brain chemistry by activating the release of neuropeptides that fight stress. Neuropeptides are tiny molecules that allow neurons (nerve cells) to communicate with each other, sending messages to the whole body when we are happy, excited, sad, angry, or depressed. When you smile, the feel-good neurotransmitters dopamine, oxytocin, serotonin, and endorphins (DOSE) are released into your system. These chemicals not only relax your body and improve your mood, but they can lower your heart rate and blood pressure as well. Dopamine is called the "motivation molecule" and boosts feelings of bliss, pleasure, and euphoria, and it also enhances drive, motivation, focus, concentration and productivity; oxytocin, known as the "cuddle hormone," provides a "warm and fuzzy" feeling; serotonin is known as the "confidence molecule" and serves as an antidepressant; and endorphins act as a natural pain reliever. Really, the solution is simple: if you want a DOSE of happiness, simply smile!

In addition to smiling, laugh often. You know what they say: "Laughter is the best medicine." It's true! Laughter increases oxygen intake and releases endorphins; it promotes heart health by lowering blood pressure and improving blood flow, thereby reducing the risk of heart attack and stroke; it strengthens immunity by boosting immune system t-cells; and laughter can lower levels of stress hormones, such as cortisol, epinephrine, and dopac. Overall, laughter makes you happy and healthy, so laugh in the face of fear and stop doubting yourself!

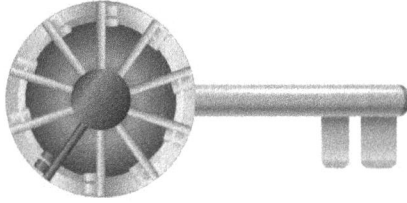

7

TRANSFORM NEGATIVES INTO POSITIVES

SAY GOODBYE TO NEGATIVE THOUGHTS, NEGATIVE ATTITUDES, AND NEGATIVE PEOPLE

"It's easy to turn a negative into a positive: just add a line." ~Nicco Boss

There are two meanings to my quote above. First, if you draw a vertical line through the middle of a minus sign, you will get a plus sign. Thus, you change a negative into a positive.

Next time you're doodling, try this: add plus signs to your artwork. I often draw hearts, stars, and flowers when I doodle, but I never forget to add my plus signs. The second way to turn a negative into a positive is by drawing on a "line" for inspiration when you're in a negative mood. If you have a favorite saying, motivational quote, or mantra, you can write down or say this line and transform your negative mood into a positive one.

Make a habit of consistently adding these positive lines to your everyday routine, and use them several times a day. When you feel yourself getting down or feeling doubtful, remember your line. It can be your one "go to" phrase that's tried and true, or you can come up with something new every time. You'll find that the more you use your line, the better you will feel, and the less often you will sense the negativity "creeping in." In fact, use the line even when you're happy and in a good frame of mind, and it will help to reinforce a consistent feeling of positivity. Bear in mind, "Don'ts don't work!" Take negative words out of your vocabulary and replace them with positive ones. Think not of what you *don't* want, but rather of what you *do* want.

In addition to using some of the longer affirmations I provided in Key 6, utilizing positive lines is tremendously helpful in bringing you into a happy mindset. Some examples of these short-but-sweet mood boosters are: *"I am enough. I am worthy. I am kind. I am needed. My life matters. I am loved."* A really great approach to constructing positive days, which translate into a positive life, is to wake up every morning with a positive thought. When you first wake up, before you even get out of bed, think a positive thought and say it out loud: *"I am alive. I am healthy. I am strong. I am confident. I am successful. I am happy."*

Even if you don't at first have confidence in some of the things you're saying, if you say them enough, you will affect your brain's neuroplasticity. This will help you to start believing the good things, and when you do this, good things happen. Your life will begin to transform in ways you never expected. Your mind is a powerful tool, and it believes what you tell it. As I explained in Key 6, your brain actually creates pathways of belief! So feed it good thoughts because from these positive seeds, beautiful flowers will grow.

Your mind doesn't just simply generate thoughts. Those thoughts produce neuropeptides, which are chemical signals in the form of messenger molecules that help your brain communicate with your body by transmitting information between the two of them. Neuropeptides are known as the "molecules of emotion" and your brain manufactures at least 100 different types of them in the hypothalamus. Your brain sends out signals that "feed" information to your body's cells, which have receptors that "eat up" what they are fed.

So, if you think sad and angry thoughts much of the time, your cells will get used to this and will end up craving sad and angry peptides. If, on the other hand, you learn to formulate happy and positive thoughts, your cells will develop an appetite for them, training your brain to think more good thoughts. These good thoughts become positive messages that are sent back into the body to feed the cells, and so on. It becomes a perpetual cycle of positivity *or* negativity, depending on how you think.

To put it into perspective, your body produces billions of new cells every hour, all of which have peptide receptors just waiting to be fed. So if you feel depressed for even one hour, you are releasing depressed peptides into your system to be consumed by the billions of new cells your body has just assembled. Naturally cells die, but not before they relay messages to the brain to create more peptides — in this case, negative ones. And the process starts all over again, creating a whirlwind in which people get trapped in their own thoughts. The negative chemicals their bodies manufacture provide adrenaline with which to fight the perceived "stressful" situation they're encountering. They actually get addicted to their stress, thereby craving it more, and thus generating still more stress to feed the addiction.

There is no denying the mind-body connection and the fact that, "What you think, you are." That's why it's important to stop the negative thinking process and instead forge neural paths of positivity. Do you want to get trapped in a cycle of complaining and program your brain to be anxious and depressed? Or would you rather develop an attitude of gratitude and promote a happy brain that feeds your body positive peptides? You have the power to make the choice and to change your life!

You must understand that the subconscious is the translator for the conscious mind, and it serves as the mirror of your life. Whatever is absorbed by your conscious mind will directly filter into your subconscious and be reflected and manifested into your existence. The subconscious doesn't distinguish between good or bad; it simply takes in the information it is given and accepts it as truth. Therefore, when you allow your negative thoughts and words to consciously enter your brain, you are permitting your subconscious to recognize the information as being valid and to do everything possible to create that reality in your life.

Along with positive affirmations, another great way to eliminate negative thoughts is to stop them in their tracks. If you notice a negative thought entering your brain, say *"STOP"* out loud. Then, physically "catch" the thought, crumple it up, and throw it away. This is where your meditation practice will come into good use because it strengthens your ability to focus. Below is a step-by-step description of this effective strategy of getting rid of negative thoughts:

Close your eyes and concentrate on the thought. See it as if it's written out on a piece of paper:

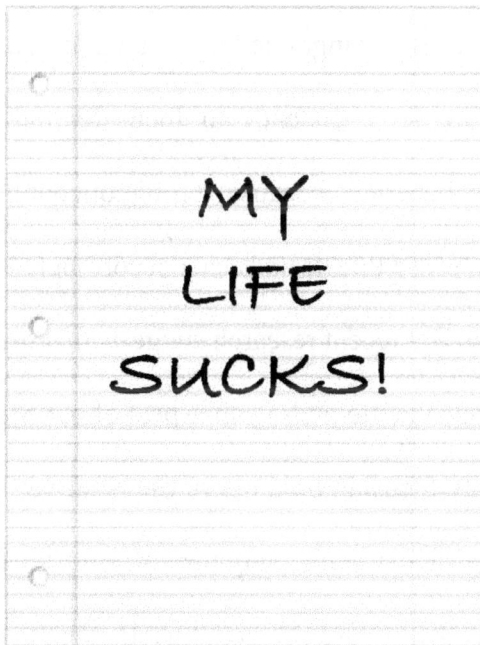

MY
LIFE
SUCKS!

Next, visualize yourself reaching out and grabbing the piece of paper. Then picture your hands crumpling up the paper into a tight ball. Now, envision yourself throwing the ball of paper into a giant wastebasket. I prefer to picture my wastebasket as a black hole because, I know that way, whatever I throw into it will be gone forever! This simple practice of throwing away bad thoughts is surprisingly impactful and extremely cathartic. It's a great technique to declutter your mind and purge yourself of emotional strain.

Negative attitudes are more difficult to change because they tend to be deeply ingrained in us. Humans have a built-in negativity bias — a tendency to focus on threats. This is evolutionarily beneficial because, throughout our history, it has enabled us to sense threats and react accordingly (often times, life-savingly). But recent research suggests that people may be able to override the life-and-death aspect of our negativity bias by consciously focusing on more of the positive. This doesn't mean that we should completely turn off our threat sensors; it simply means that we are able to adjust to what the real threats are in our modern world. After all, we no longer have to worry about fighting off saber-toothed tigers!

We are all born as a blank slate, with no thoughts, ideas, opinions, or prejudices. It is through our upbringing that we develop our belief systems. We are molded by our parents and extended family, our friends, our physical environment, our geographical location, our educational system, our cultural influences, our religious beliefs, our work environment, and the list goes on. It's no wonder we have so many conflicting thoughts and feelings, and it's no surprise that we fall victim to negative attitudes in life. Our brains are so overwhelmed with mixed messages and crossed signals, I believe it's only a matter of time before everyone starts to short-circuit!

But there is a method to prevent a mass breakdown in society: it is to change your attitude. Everyone has the capacity to reverse negative attitudes by adopting positive ones. It may be a gradual process, depending upon how deeply you've fallen into the trenches of darkness. But it is possible to alter your perceptions in life — whether they be about people, things, or just life in general — in favor of a more optimistic outlook.

The ideal manner of changing your attitudes about other people is to "put yourself in their shoes." You don't know what someone is feeling unless you find out what they are going through, and the simplest approach is to ask! Discover more about people and their life stories. Find out why they do things a certain way: why they dress as they do, or eat the foods they eat, or practice certain customs. Understand the reasons behind their uniqueness. You'll be surprised to learn that other people are not as different from you as you thought. On a fundamental level, every person of every color, ethnicity, race, and religion has the one same desire: *TO BE HAPPY!*

And your happiness starts with you! You cannot depend on anyone to bring you joy and contentment. Sure, there are some people who make you happy when you're around them. You should spend as much time with those people as possible because they build upon your foundational well-being. Just as this is true, you should avoid negative people as much as possible. If you encounter bad feelings or sad emotions around certain people, it is your body's mechanism of telling you they're no good. Follow your intuition — it's one of your most powerful resources! Human beings are born with excellent natural instincts. Unfortunately, we tend to ignore them too often because we want to believe that people are good, or that a situation will turn out for the best. Don't believe it! Remember those "gut instincts" from Key 4? Learn to listen to them! If you have uneasy feelings about a person, or if you feel completely drained after spending time with someone, do yourself a favor and say goodbye. You will be better off, and you'll notice immediately how much better you feel.

You might say, "But the negative person in my life is my sister/dad/cousin. I can't just cut them out of my life." In most cases this is true, but you can distance yourself from the naysayer. Don't spend as much time as you usually would with that person. On holidays or at family reunions, be friendly and stay positive. If Negative Ned or Debbie Downer accosts you with a hostile remark or tries to rope you into their pity party (or what I like to call a "commiseration celebration"), counter with a positive comment and politely excuse yourself to find a happier place at the gathering. They will be so caught off-guard by your response that they won't quite know what to do. You'll find that if you consistently react to negative people in this manner, they will either stop being negative around you, or they will leave you alone altogether. You see, negative people enjoy confronting others in an attempt to get a reaction. "Misery loves company," as they say, and if you don't commiserate with these people, they'll go elsewhere to find like-minded people. Don't worry, it's really no loss for you because a negative loss is a positive gain — and that's another way to turn a negative into a positive!

It's really not that difficult to become an optimist and look for the positive in every situation. If you learn how to look, you'll start to see the silver lining in just about anything. All it takes is one good thought to start the positive-thinking ball rolling, and once it gains momentum, you'll find it hard to stop. This is because your brain is a positive feedback loop, and usually just one small shift in thinking will jump-start it into a

Positivity Cycle:

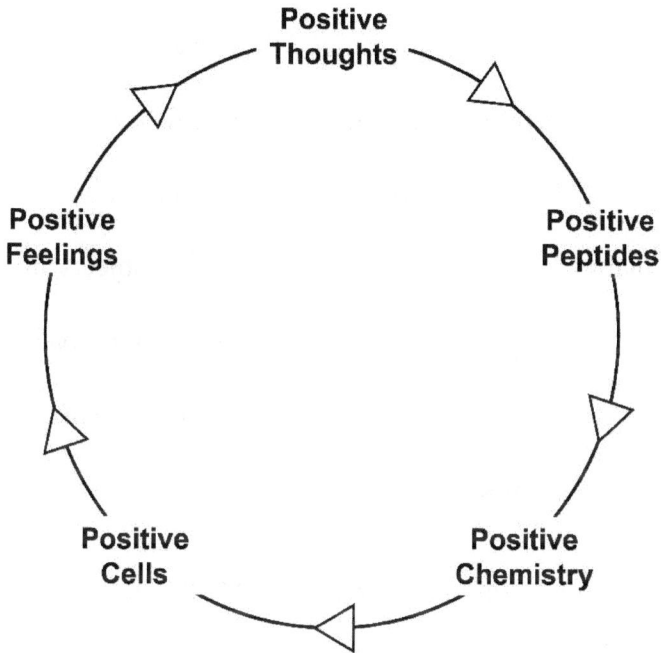

```
                    Positive
                    Thoughts

   Positive                        Positive
   Feelings                        Peptides



   Positive                        Positive
    Cells                         Chemistry
```

You see, it's actually pretty easy to start a cycle of positive

thinking. There is *always* a bright side — you just can't forget

to take your blinders off and let the light shine in!

Speaking of light shining in, sometimes the cracks in our lives *are* the beauty of our experience. Have you ever considered that a broken heart is a good thing? *YES!* It's through the cracks in our heart that we are able to allow true love to flood in. It is only through the experience of knowing "bad love" which has hurt us that we can find "true love" which can heal us. Look at the flaws or blemishes in your life as the parts that make you special. In Japan, broken objects are often repaired with gold. The flaw is seen as a unique part of the object's history, which adds to its beauty. Please remember this when you feel broken.

Being an optimist doesn't mean that you always see the glass as half full, and it doesn't mean you can't feel sad or angry sometimes, or even negative! It just means that even when you're feeling down, you can see the good in a situation. By training your mind to do this, you won't let difficult situations affect you so deeply. When you make optimism a habit, you will bounce back from adversity much more quickly and easily.

The happiest people aren't void of negativity; they just choose to focus more on the positive.

There will be days when you just don't feel positive, *period*, and that's okay! You are human, after all. The key is to build gradually to having more positive thoughts and saying more positive words than negative. By taking a slow but steady approach to enlightenment, you are constructing a more solid and realistic foundation to long-lasting success. So, for example, if someone asks you how you are doing, and you feel like crap, don't say, "Fine." But also try not to say, "I feel like crap!" Instead, say something more positive-*leaning*, such as, "I'm sure it'll turn out to be a great day;" or "Feeling better every minute;" or "Working on my to-do list." By doing this, you're being open to the possibility — and actively creating the probability — of having a good day.

This is what is called *creating your own reality*. Even if you aren't feeling all that great when you wake up, you have a choice about how your day will actually come to pass. You decide how you will feel by expressing yourself in one of two ways: positively, or negatively. It's really that simple. To *feel* happy, you must express yourself with happy words; and to speak happily, you must think positively. To think positively, you have to believe in yourself. A good procedure to strengthen your self-belief is to practice meditation and repeat positive affirmations or mantras so that they are embedded in your subconscious mind. You must establish goals for yourself and do everything possible to achieve them. Be grateful for everything you have and say "thank you" often. Observe your emotions, and if you're not feeling happy, remember to focus on the present moment. By ignoring your doubts and fears and actively transforming negatives into positives, you bring yourself to the point where you can actually effect a significant change in your life. After you put Keys 1 through 7 into practice, you will be ready for the next Key step: *ACTION!*

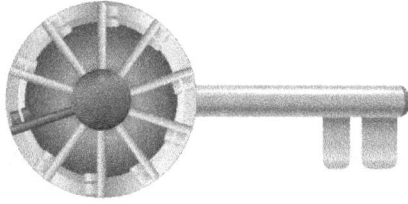

8

INITIATE CHANGE THROUGH ACTION

YOU CAN'T MOVE FORWARD WHILE YOU'RE STANDING STILL

"Dreams don't work unless you do."
~John C. Maxwell

As I mentioned in Key 7, you must take action toward what you want in life. Maybe you've heard the expression, "Ask, Believe, Receive." Well, that's a nice assertion, but if you never set a ball in motion, it won't ever move. This is expressed by Newton's First Law of Motion: *An object at rest will remain at rest unless a force acts upon it, and an object in motion will not change its velocity unless acted upon by an unbalanced force.*

The key to getting what you want in life is to take the proper action steps toward your goals. You may be familiar with the concept of the "Law of Attraction," which states that you will attract to yourself whatever you focus on in your life. The basic principle is "like attracts like," meaning that if you think about good things and maintain happy thoughts, good and positive things will come to you. Alternatively, if you think about bad things and focus on the negative, you will be attracting these things into your life.

The philosophy of the Law of Attraction is very similar to the idea of positive thinking, in that both put forth the notion that what you focus on will be manifested in your life. Positive thinking has been scientifically proven to change your brain's neuroplasticity and your body's chemistry, improving health and increasing happiness. The action of focusing on positive thoughts will produce the desired results. However, if you're expecting a new car to magically appear in your garage just by asking for it and believing you'll get it, you'll be in for a big surprise when you look out to see your old lemon waiting to take you on your daily commute. It's okay to believe in the Law of Attraction, but if you're going to practice it in an effort to get something you want, I would definitely add one vital step to the motto associated with the Law: **A**sk, **B**elieve, *Act*, **R**eceive (*ABAR*). You can ask, believe, think, feel, and hope all you want, but if you don't *act* upon your desires, you'll never get what you're looking for.

You can fantasize about your dream partner every day for years, but if you don't leave your house, you will never find them (unless you fall in love with your parcel delivery person!). So get the ball rolling. Usually, it takes the smallest first step, and once you begin, you'll see that it's easier than you thought and what you're after is closer than you know! By focusing positively on what you desire, you are opening your subconscious to finding solutions where you couldn't perceive them with your conscious mind; and by moving forward, you are uncovering options you would never have had by just staying in the same place. Standing still leads to stagnation!

Besides the fear of the unknown, there are many reasons we become paralyzed into inaction: we don't believe in ourselves, we don't have faith in others, we fear rejection, we fear success, we fear failure, and we just can't bear to face one more disappointment. Sometimes, the familiarity of your situation is much easier to live with. Or sometimes you know what you want, and you believe you can have it, so you ask for it and actually follow through with action … but still, nothing seems to happen. You ask, you believe, you feel, you *ACT* — but *still* you don't receive! So what's the problem? The issue is that you're blocking your own desires! Sounds crazy, right? It's not.

You may not even realize this, but many of us are closing ourselves off from all of the good things and happiness we want and deserve. Subconsciously, we don't allow things in because we are so used to protecting ourselves from being hurt — especially if we've lived through a lot of painful experiences. As a result, not only are we blocking the "bad" things, but we are also blocking the "good." Think about how often you stand with your arms crossed. Most times, this is an unconscious act of self-protection that you are completely unaware of. Pay attention to how you stand the next time you're waiting in line for something or even hanging out with friends. Sure, sometimes it's more comfortable to stand with your arms crossed, but more often than not, you're shielding yourself. (Or you could just be cold, and then it's okay!)

To get what you want, and to truly benefit from all that life has to offer, you must thoroughly accept every circumstance. All of our life experiences are beneficial, even those we perceive as "bad," because each and every thing we live through brings value into our existence. Every situation provides us with a learning lesson from which to become stronger and more knowledgeable, or it offers us guidance in moving forward on the right path. Accept all of your experiences with an open mind, for you never know where the twists and turns may lead you. Often what we perceive as rejection is merely redirection toward something bigger and better.

The secret to getting what you want is to remain open to receiving. Remember, with an open heart we feel more fully, with open eyes we see more clearly, and with open arms we receive more abundantly. In all, we gain depth, clarity, and well-being. So always keep an open mind and be grateful for every life lesson and gift that happens to appear. When opportunity comes knocking, don't forget to open the door!

The way to encourage all of the goodness and opportunities for happiness to enter your life is to set your intention. Say to yourself, *"I am open to receiving all that I ask for, believe in, and work toward with good intention. I am grateful for ALL of my life experiences: the 'good' ones for opening my heart, and the 'bad' ones for opening my eyes."* With your sincere determination to being open to receiving what the Universe has to offer, you are sure to be presented with gifts even greater than you could have dreamed possible! But don't forget to feel gratitude when you get what you were wishing for. The happiest people are not those who simply get what they want, but those who appreciate and enjoy what they get!

Another very important action step that we can all take in our lives in our pursuit of happiness is the way we actually perceive happiness itself. Sometimes people mistake happiness with material possessions or personal accomplishments; however, these things are often short-lived, leaving us even more unfulfilled and dissatisfied once we achieve our goals. The key is to understand *happiness* versus *meaning* in life.

Does that new outfit bring you true happiness? Maybe the first few times you wear it, and when it shrinks and fades and goes out of style, you probably won't like it anymore. Or what about that shiny new car — that's sure to bring you continuing happiness, right? Well, that joy may last a little longer, until the novelty wears off and you have to pay for costly upkeep and repairs. Even the thrill of living in a brand new house fades once the responsibilities of maintenance, as well as the grind of daily life, set in.

The way we adjust to any new circumstance in our lives is a prime reason we cannot find enduring happiness in outside sources; it's called "hedonic adaptation." Human beings are incredibly adept at getting used to changes in our life circumstances and sensory experiences. Even if we've spent years pursuing something, once we finally get it, we adapt to it rather quickly. No matter what positive, thrilling, and wonderful event happens to us, when we become habituated to something, it becomes boring, and we're left wanting more. Monotony takes us right back to our baseline of happiness, which is the overall average level of subjective well-being we feel in our lives.

There are two methods to diminish the effects of hedonic adaptation: 1) change routines often, and 2) find meaning in everything you do. Obviously, we all have a general daily routine that we must follow in our lives because most of us work and/or go to school. But try mixing up things that are not set by time or other constraints. Instead of having Taco Tuesday every week, make it every other week; or (gasp!) have

Taco Wednesday. That's right, learn to live life on the edge! If you normally do laundry every Sunday, change it to Saturday, and make Sunday a day to relax. If you only ever go jogging, try bicycling for a change. Instead of meeting your friends at the same coffee shop every morning, switch it up and visit a new place. Changing routines every once in a while will help to keep things feeling fresh and new. Even the smallest changes can break the tedium of everyday life.

The other way to combat falling into a pattern of habituation is to set your intention on living a *meaningful* life, rather than just a *happy* one. The difference between the two is that people who wish to live a happy life are often seeking to satisfy their wants and needs, rather than striving to find the meaning and purpose that their lives hold. Living a meaningful life takes into account living in the present by applying what you have experienced in your past and looking forward to all of the potential of your future. It incorporates living your life as a complete unit and understanding that doing so will make you whole. People who live *meaningful* lives understand that life is not only about happy or positive experiences, but the sum of all situations that allow for absolute growth.

People who are most content and, therefore, "happy" in their lives derive meaning through helping others and knowing that all life is connected. Simply stated, if we feel that we are leading meaningful lives, we will automatically feel happy. Most people feel happiest when they have a purpose and are fulfilling that reason for living. Thus, meaningfulness creates the most genuine and lasting happiness of all. This is known as "eudaimonic happiness," which comes from meaningful pursuits. This is in direct contrast with "hedonic happiness," which comes from pleasure or goal fulfilments. This type of happiness leads to the hedonic adaptation that I described before, creating a never-ending cycle of needing more and more, yet never feeling satisfied.

If you make only one change in the way you strive for happiness, it would be to take inspired action toward meaningful pursuits. It's not wrong to want to live a comfortable life with material possessions. But if your sole ambition is to live a life full of self-indulgence, then you will never find yourself on the path to true happiness. You will forever be on a roller coaster seeking your next high, instead of living on a steady stream of meaningful significance. The question is: *How would you rather live?*

9

Visualize Your Purpose and Dreams

If You Pursue Your Passion, You Will Find Your Purpose

"The purpose in life is to be happy....Compassion is the pathway to happiness."
~ The Dalai Lama

I believe that each and every one of us has the right to happiness. But I also believe that the purpose of life is a life full of purpose. Mark Twain famously said, "The two most important days in your life are the day you are born and the day you find out why." If you follow your purpose, everything else in your life will fall into place.

What if you don't know what your purpose is? There is a simple answer to this: do what you love in life and love what you do. If you follow your heart and pursue your passion, you won't have to search for your life's purpose — it will find you. But you must stay positive in order to be open to all possibilities that life has to offer. This is how you will attract a life full of goodness and meaning. There is no mistaking the feeling of joy and fulfillment that comes from aligning yourself with your true purpose in the world. The key is to visualize your dreams.

Everyone knows how to visualize — basically, visualizing is just multidimensional thinking, vibrant and colorful. We learned how to visualize early on in our lives as children when we played make-believe. Fantasizing and daydreaming are actually very healthy aspects of life. Evoking a pleasant memory or creating an image that fills us with excitement is enough to activate the release of oxytocin. In fact, utilizing the tool of visualization can generate as much oxytocin in the body as physical touch! Unfortunately, as we get older, we are told that daydreaming is bad. We are led to believe that it takes us away from reality and from our responsibilities. Have you ever heard adults say, "Quit daydreaming. You're going to waste your life away!" I am here to tell you to daydream more! Daydreaming is essentially a form of meditation, which is one of the most effective and powerful forms of attaining peace and, as a result, becoming more productive.

We often hear the expression, "Follow your heart." We all know that this means to follow your dreams and passion. When making life choices, it is always important to do what you intuitively feel is right, or what you truly want, deep down. Sometimes, we are met with conflicting feelings because we have obligations to a job, spouse, school, children, aging parents, etc., and we often take ourselves last. It is so critical *NOT* to do this. You must make it a point to feed your soul *first*, even if it's just for ten minutes a day. When we are whole, we have the ability to give to others.

In life we are required to make choices on a daily basis. In fact, it is said that adults make a staggering 35,000 "remotely conscious" decisions every day! (In contrast, children make only about 3,000.) Of course, many of the choices we make involve things like what to eat and what to wear, but countless others are extremely important and can have impactful effects on our lives. Examples include career choices, options about if, when, and whom to marry, determinations about our children's future, financial decisions, and questions over whether to fulfill obligations to other people — just to name a few. It's so overwhelming, it's no wonder we sometimes feel as if we don't have all the answers.

But I must impress upon you that you do have all the answers inside. You already know what to do, so trust your inner guidance and follow it. You must simply ***tune in to your intuition***, and you will find all of the answers you are looking for. Think of intuition as *teaching* (tuition) *from within* (in).

This is where meditating becomes essential. By going inside and tuning into your subconscious, you block out the noise and distractions that are preventing you from finding the truth.

If you are still having trouble making a decision, a really great strategy to know what you sincerely desire deep down is to flip a coin. Yes, you read that right! I'm not telling you to let major life choices be decided by a coin toss. Instead, the coin just helps you realize what it is that you really want. Assign different options in how to proceed in a situation, or answers (such as "yes" or "no"), to each side of the coin. Then, while flipping the coin, ask your question out loud. For example, "Should I stay at my job (heads), or should I pursue my dream career (tails)?" or "Should I stay with this person?" or "Is moving the right thing to do?" Before the coin even shows you the answer, your heart will tell you what to do, because whichever side of the coin you are wishing to see is exactly what you want to happen. And that, my friends, is what you call following your heart!

A similar scenario occurs when you ask a friend or family member for advice. They tell you what they think you should do, and you totally disagree with them. Then they say, "Why did you even ask me in the first place if you already knew what you wanted to do?" This happens to everyone, and it's a good thing (except when it causes problems between you and the person whose advice you're soliciting). It's good because — just like the coin toss — it's a method for you to confirm what you already know and want deep down. It just feels better when you have that confirmation!

Following your heart and trusting your intuition is the best way to live. By doing so, you will always find the answers you are seeking — the *right* answers. If you learn how to observe your emotions and follow your instincts, the easiest path will always open up for you. The key is to go inside yourself (meditation), let go of resistance, stay positive, and allow life to flow. Only then will you bring to light your true purpose and reason for being. Too often, people end up doing something that's completely wrong for them because it's what they're told to do, or they think it's what society expects of them — and that leads to unhappiness. If you are living a life that other people want you to live, you are wasting your purpose. Your true fulfillment comes from being who you are meant to be, and only you can discover that.

One simple way to find your purpose is to think about instances in your life when time seemed to fly by. Have you ever been so positively engaged in an endeavor that you lost track of time? This state of being "in the zone" is what psychologists call *flow*, and it is defined as "an intrinsically rewarding or optimal state that results from intense engagement with daily activities."

Everyone can think of the fun times when they felt like they were in a state of flow: celebrating a birthday, being on vacation, spending time with loved ones, watching an entertaining movie, enjoying a delicious meal, and so on. You're probably thinking, "Sure, it's easy to find flow when you're doing something fun! But what about when you're working?" Believe it or not, a lot of people love their work, and that's a crucial secret to happiness. Pinpoint what you love to do, and do that as much as possible. Try to incorporate it into your career. If you like to paint, paint; if you savor cooking, cook; if you enjoy crunching numbers, by all means, crunch away; if you have a green thumb, try gardening; and if you have a blue thumb, become a smurf!

Engaging in pursuits that promote flow enhances happiness. When you are in flow, your concentration is at its highest level, and you are unable to be distracted. Three signs that you are in flow are: 1) you are sufficiently challenged so as not to lose interest in the activity; 2) you are able to adapt to changes easily and seamlessly; and 3) you really enjoy what you're doing. We are able to achieve a state of flow when we do things voluntarily; it's about the things we *choose* to do and *love* to do.

Another important factor in achieving flow is your environment. First, you have to be doing something within your own skill set. If you select something too easy, you'll get bored; if something's too hard, you'll become frustrated and be more likely to quit. Next, your objectives must be clear, and you need to be receiving consistent feedback about how close you are to accomplishing them. Finally, you must be free to fully concentrate on your task.

Discovering your flow will help you to find your passion, and pursuing your passion will lead you right to your purpose. Let your intuition guide you to your true heart's desire, and you will find a deeper sense of joy and a higher level of elation than just ordinary happiness. This is because when you are guided by the power of the wisdom within you, you will achieve a life that is full of meaning and bliss, and *that* is the pinnacle of happiness!

Take the Keys I have taught you here and realize your destiny. Step by step and day by day, your life will unfold magically, the unnecessary layers dropping off and ridding you of the burdensome weight you have been carrying. When you no longer bear the heaviness of the unwanted roles you've been assigned with, you are free to fly to limitless heights.

Perhaps your purpose in life is to help others. I hold the strong opinion that it is everyone's responsibility in life to help others to a certain extent. Mahatma Gandhi said, "The best way to find yourself is to lose yourself in the service of others." I believe this to be so true because, in helping others, we find our compassion and build our empathy. Becoming more empathetic helps us to develop our understanding of others, and by comprehending others better, we appreciate ourselves more fully. Augmented empathy can lead to significant increases in happiness.

Empathy is not just a mode of expanding our moral boundaries. New research shows that it's a habit we can all cultivate to improve the quality of our lives. Being empathetic involves having the ability to step into another person's shoes with the intent of understanding their feelings and outlook on life, and to use that understanding to conduct our own actions.

When you learn to associate with others, you develop a connection with them, which leads to stronger and more meaningful social interactions. According to neuroscientific studies, when people form bonds by sharing experiences and supporting others in life, there is greater activation of their dopamine reward circuitry. This proves that we are capable of feeling as much (or more) joy, achievement, and pleasure from helping others as if we do something for ourselves. There's also the increased likelihood that others will empathize with your pain and suffering and support you!

Empathy, kindness, and compassion for others provide happiness, satisfaction, and overall better health. One Emory University study recorded participants' brain activity while they were helping others. The remarkable finding was that being of service to others triggered activity in the portions of the brain that turn on when people receive rewards or experience pleasure. Therefore, practicing kindness by doing things for others brings us the same pleasure we get from the gratification of personal desire. It's true that the act of giving and feeling happiness reinforce each other, creating a positive feedback loop. How ironic that in helping others, we help ourselves!

Does that make helping others a selfish act? Not at all! It's a win-win situation in the best sense, especially if helping others can help you find your true calling. After all, pursuing your passion and finding your purpose are essential to living a happy, fulfilled life. If you're still having trouble finding your true place in this world, and you feel that the answers are eluding you, maybe you just need to learn how to decipher the codes.

Perhaps the answers are all right in front of you, but you don't know how to interpret them. This is where learning comes into play. You won't understand a foreign language unless you study it. Similarly, you can't move toward genuine happiness until you understand how. Part of the process includes following the Keys I have laid out in this book, the last one being quite possibly the most important. Knowledge will propel you to levels of awareness that will uncover your bliss. There are many forms of education that come from various sources, but no matter how you gain it, know that knowledge is powerful!

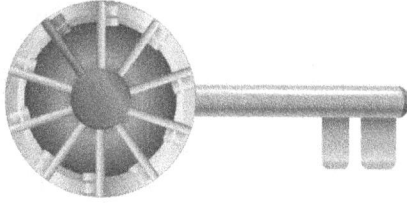

10

EMPOWER YOURSELF WITH KNOWLEDGE

KNOWLEDGE IS THE KEY TO SUCCESS

"Knowledge itself is power." ~Sir Francis Bacon
(Meditationes Sacrae 1597)

Feelings of fear and confusion stem from a lack of information. If you find yourself being indecisive and unable to focus on your intentions, don't create more stress in your life by worrying. Instead, take the time to inform yourself by seeking the knowledge that will empower you and elevate you to a higher level of awareness. The more you know, the better able you will be to put yourself in a position of security and confidence in life. When you feel confident in your abilities and secure with yourself, you will automatically be happier.

Acquiring knowledge will benefit you in any and every area of your life because being well-informed will help you to make better choices. Obviously, it's important to educate yourself in fields of study that will help you to advance through life in positive, prepared ways. But being knowledgeable in the book sense is only one realm of study in which you should invest.

The most worthwhile subject in which to educate yourself is: *YOU*. Aristotle said, "Knowing yourself is the beginning of all wisdom." Embark on earning a Master's Degree in "*The Study of Me*" and you will soon hold the answers to any questions you might have about how to navigate through your life. After all, the relationship you have with yourself is the most significant one you'll ever have in your whole life.

If you don't fully know yourself, how do expect others to understand you? Garnering knowledge of who you are will help you to build a healthy self-esteem and will lead to a more fulfilling life. The only true method of lifting yourself to a higher level of well-being is to know yourself inside and out, forward, backward, upside down, and right-side-up! You have to know yourself so well that the moment something throws you off balance or knocks you down, you are able to immediately take action to correct the problem and get right back up.

The first step in getting to really know yourself is to learn your happiness set point and be able to formulate where it falls on a scale from one to ten. Your *happiness set point* is the level of your subjective well-being as determined mainly by genetics, personality traits, and habits that have been instilled in you from early on. It's basically a "happiness continuum" you're born with that remains relatively constant throughout your life and does not usually change as a result of exterior circumstances. However, new discoveries reveal that, by changing our interior landscape through training the mind, we can actually raise our happiness set point number!

Once you have a good idea of what your baseline happiness set point number is, you'll be able to measure your happiness at any given time and take steps to adjust it. No one is at a 10 level of happiness all the time. In fact, some people never reach level 10 because maybe their genetic happiness barometer hovers at around level 6 or 7. It's important to establish this because once you know where your baseline is, it's much easier to take steps to get back to that number if you've dipped below it. In many cases, you can actually implement techniques to increase it!

We all come into the world with a genetically determined "set point" for happiness. Some people are intrinsically happier than others — they're just born that way. Studies have revealed that identical twins are more similar in their levels of happiness than fraternal twins. This suggests that happiness is heritable, or passed down through families. It has been ascertained that 50% of the state of our happiness is genetically determined. So how do you become happier if you were born into a family of pessimists? That's where the other 50% comes in.

In addition to our 50% of genetic happiness, we can factor in 10% from life circumstances and 40% from intentional activity. *WHAT?* A whopping forty percent of our happiness comes from what we have control over in our lives? *YES!* Through our own intentions, we have the power to change our overall feeling of well-being. Without a doubt, your happiness is under your command, so you really have no excuse for prolonged unhappiness. But how do you enhance your joy and maximize your baseline level of happiness? By implementing the Keys I have given you in this book. Also, I have created this ***Happiness Formula*** for you to use to help you assess your happiness reference point:

$$(G \times .5) + (LC \times .1) + (IA \times .4) = H$$

G = Genetics, LC = Life Circumstances

IA = Intentional Activity, H = Happiness

Your genetics **(G)** determine your ***happiness set point***; your life circumstances **(LC)** added to your genetics number give you your ***happiness benchmark***; and these two numbers added to your intentional activity **(IA)** provide you with your overall ***happiness number***. By using this formula to discover your reference point of happiness, you can actually raise your number (i.e. your happiness) according to how you apply the Keys in this book.

As I mentioned before, you first have to ascertain what your genetic happiness set point is. Assign yourself a number between 1 and 10 that describes your broad sense of well-being, based on your genes, family history, upbringing, and personality. You have to be honest with yourself when assessing your personal traits or characteristics — don't say you're a 10 if you're constantly complaining about every little thing in life.

Are you a generally happy person? Are you enthusiastic about life? Hopeful? Cautiously optimistic? Or are you indifferent? Skeptical? Sardonic? It's okay if your genetic set point is a 5 or a 6; that just means you'll have to work a little

bit harder at your daily intentional activity in order to increase

your baseline. By understanding your natural personality traits

and establishing your set point, you can always, with conscious

effort, lift yourself to greater heights.

Once you have a good idea of what your happiness set

point is, you will be able to evaluate your overall happiness (or

well-being), relative to that number, at any given time. First, on

a scale from one to ten, rate your well-being as measured

against your current life circumstances. If your job is great and

you have awesome friends, but you can't seem to find your

soulmate, you might say your level of contentedness is a 6 or a

7. If you have a wonderful marriage and beautiful kids, but you

feel stuck in a dead-end job, maybe you'd say your well-being

is an 8. Or maybe you just lost your job and your spouse has

left you, and your friends have told you that it's all your fault;

in this situation, you might rate your optimism a 3 (let's hope

this isn't the case!). You can rate your well-being daily,

weekly, or monthly — whatever gives you the clearest sense of your happiness level.

When you have an average calculation of your benchmark happiness number according to your genetics and life circumstances, you can devise the best plan regarding what changes you could make in your life — through intentional activity — in order to improve that number. This will give you your comprehensive, or overall, happiness number.

Let's work out an example. Say you're from a very merry family; you would rate your Genetics (G) happiness set point number at 8. Next, if you've been through an average experience of challenges in your life, you'd probably rate your Life Circumstances (LC) number at 5. Finally, you determine that you don't do too much about practicing gratitude, having self-compassion, or living in the present moment, etc., so you decide that your Intentional Activity (IA) number is at a 6. Plug the numbers into the formula [8 x .5 = 4; 5 x .1 = .5; 6 x .4 = 2.4] and add the results to get your overall happiness number: 4 + .5 + 2.4 = 6.9. This isn't too bad on a scale from 1 to 10, but there's definitely room for improvement. That's where practicing all of the Keys I have presented in this book will help to elevate your happiness to a higher level.

Pursuits that will increase your level of cheerfulness in life include any (or all) of the exercises I have presented in this book. By *B*elieving in yourself, *E*stablishing goals, *P*racticing gratitude, *O*bserving your emotions, *S*taying in the present moment, *I*gnoring your doubts and fears, *T*ransforming negatives into positives, *I*nitiating change through action, *V*isualizing your purpose and dreams, and *E*mpowering yourself with knowledge, you are making a conscious effort toward creating and maintaining your well-being.

Now that I have presented to you these ten important Keys in creating your true happiness, I am going to give you one final ***FUNDAMENTAL KEY: BE CONSISTENT!*** No matter what you aim to accomplish in life, the one common denominator of success is consistency. You won't lose weight if you diet for a week and then give up; you won't master a new skill if you quit applying yourself after a month; and you won't generate everlasting happiness if you "try" for a little while, thinking that what you do for a few weeks or months will stick. If you want to see positive change in your life, you must be the one to effect that change. Only you have the power to make yourself happy, and that comes from a conscious decision to make happiness a way of life.

By choosing to read this book, you have already taken the first step in realizing your true purpose in life, which is to be happy! Always keep in mind that **HAPPINESS** is your birthright, so don't ever let anyone take that away from you. If you need to find answers, the first step is to go inside yourself and seek solutions from within. Listen to your intuition telling you that you are already enough. Learn to embrace all that you are, because you are perfection in all your imperfections.

Sometimes we need reassurance to remember this. It can be very helpful to supplement with information from books or guidance from mentors and advisers. Often, it is through our own life experiences that we gain invaluable knowledge. Take what you have learned from the past and build upon those lessons to create a stronger future.

Work on positive intention, and frame life goals in positive terms only. Value yourself and your actions, as opposed to expecting someone else to affirm you. Let go of the idea of "becoming someone," because you are already a masterpiece. Release the need for acceptance from others; accept and love yourself just as you are. It is much more important for you to feel good about yourself than for others to feel good about you. Besides, when you love and respect yourself, you'll attract people who treat you the same way.

Life doesn't always serve up perfect conditions for happiness. However, when you are swimming in a sea of positivity, a few drops of negativity won't disrupt the balance. When you radiate light, a few dark words won't be able to overshadow your joy. When you know who you are and what you have to offer, and when you arrive at being unconditionally content with your very existence, nothing and no one can ever take your happiness away!

Wishing You

Happiness Always!

Nicco Boss

==

For more Information, Inspiration, and Motivation,

please subscribe at:

www.NiccoBoss.com

==

Resources

National Suicide Prevention Lifeline: 1-800-273-8255 (24hrs/day) SuicidePreventionLifeline.org

Association for Psychological Science: psychologicalscience.org

BiologicalPsychiatryJournal.com

Carnegie Mellon University: cmu.edu

ETH Zürich: ethz.ch

Feinstein Institute for Medical Research: feinsteininstitute.org

Greater Good Science Center: greatergood.berkeley.edu

Harvard University: harvard.edu

Journal of Neuroscience: jneurosci.org

MedicineNet.com

National Center for Complementary and Integrative Health: nccih.nih.gov

PsychologyToday.com

ScienceDirect.com

University of California, Berkeley: berkeley.edu

University of Massachusetts Medical Center: umassmed.edu

University of North Carolina at Chapel Hill: unc.edu

University of Rochester Medical Center: urmc.rochester.edu

VeryWell.com

Index

About the Author

Nicco Boss is a multi-genre writer, Life and Happiness Coach, motivational speaker, and mentor. Like most people, she has endured her share of adversity in life. Tragedy found its way into her life story at the tender age of 14 months, when her father was killed in a car accident by a drunk driver. Over the ensuing years, she has grieved the loss of loved ones to various causes (including suicide), battled a life-threatening illness, and struggled through the ordeals of divorce.

Despite all of this, Nicco persevered, withstood the hardships, and summoned the courage to pick herself up and emerge stronger and happier than ever! How did she do it? By living and learning, going through a whole lot of trial and error, and — most crucial of all — *never* giving up hope and *always* staying positive. She remained determined to transform adversity into advantage.

As a result of the sum of her personal experiences, formal education, and lifelong acquisition of knowledge, Nicco has uncovered a path to well-being and has dedicated her life to sharing it with others. From tragedy to triumph, she has discovered the **KEY TO HAPPINESS: POSITIVIKEY**.

Nicco Boss resides in Las Vegas with her two sons.

NOTES